Hans Hayden's Nürmbergisch Geigenwerk (after Praetorius)

Hanns Neupert

Harpsichord Manual

A historical and technical discussion

English Translation by F.E. Kirby

Second Edition

Bärenreiter Kassel · Basel · Paris · London · New York

1968

Translated from the fourth German Edition

TABLE OF CONTENTS

PREFACE TO THE SECOND AND THIRD EDITIONS

Since 1932, when I completed the first edition of this work, interest in harpsichords has not lessened but rather has increased, as much in connection with the performance of the music of earlier periods as in arousing interest in new compositions for the instrument. In the difficult years preceding, during and following the war this revival naturally suffered severe setbacks through the loss of men who were dedicated pioneers as well as through the destruction of countless instruments and irreplacable literature. Even in post-war years the growth of this movement will have many obstacles with which to contend. But, in any case, it has not ceased to exist; on the contrary, it has maintained itself and has much to contribute to our musical culture by virtue of its preoccupation with timeless values, the intimate character of its music and music making, as well as its qualities of good craftsmanship.

May the present little monograph on harpsichords, originally conceived only as a guide to the harpsichord owners, in its new edition contribute to the knowledge, the appreciation and the advancement of the harpsichord and in this way serve a harpsichord revival which is not a flight from the present but a source of energy for the future.

Bamberg, August, 1946 and 1955 Hanns Neupert

INTRODUCTION

The early music is still alive! This fact can no longer be taken as a mere transitory fashion, as the curious habit of a few isolated music lovers, or as a dealing in antiques totally out of step with the times. It must rather be seen as a logical and consequent development that the renaissance of our musical culture has brought new life to early music instruments. Music, if it is really to live again, must sound and this, in turn, requires the proper medium for performance. It is indeed possible to use modern instruments for the performance of old and pre-classic music, but this is a mere substitute, a transplanting on foreign soil. Today we know something of that mysterious affinity between the music itself and the technique in the construction of instruments, by which, in all periods of music history, the potentialities of the instruments to sound go hand in hand with the goals of musical expression, so that the musical ideal of each period requires its specific medium, peculiar to it alone. Thus, the spirit and form of early music, if it is really to be revived, require the proper sound media in order to remain true to the music itself and to maintain purity in style. The revival of the music of early times, therefore, could not go without influence on the construction of instruments.

The procession of early musical instruments brought to new life was begun by the harpsichord, followed by the viola da gamba, the viola d'amore, the lute, the baroque organ, the recorder, the vielle, etc. In accordance with its important position among these early instruments, the harpsichord, whixh has not been totally eclipsed by its modern successor, the piano, and its whole family of related instruments, should be taken by itself and treated more thoroughly than has yet been done in the literature on musical instruments.

Together with an historical discussion the author will take up the construction of early harpsichords and questions relating to modern instrument building, which fall close to his own province of activity.

FAMILY TREE OF THE PIANO

(From H. Neupert: Vom Musikstab zum modernen Klavier)

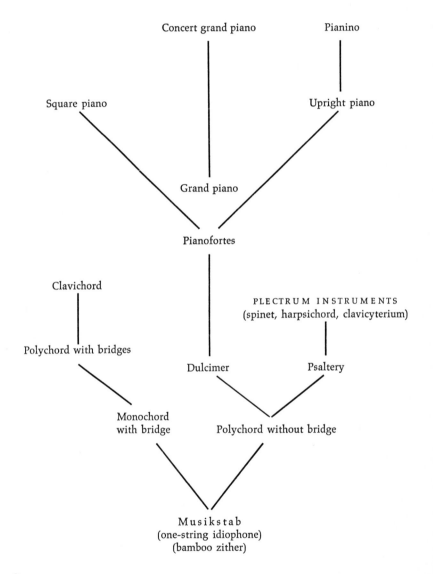

GENERAL DISCUSSION OF THE HARPSICHORD FAMILY

To obtain a clear picture of the origin and early forms of the harpsichord it is not necessary for us to go back to the very roots of the keyboard instrument family tree, but we can proceed directly to the Middle Ages —around the year 1300—to a time when the stringed instruments descended from the *Musikstab* had developed to the point at which they could be made to produce a tone by means of a mechanical action of some sort. (Here the addition of levers designed to make a body of strings to sound; it is not until the addition of the key (Latin, *clavis*) that we really have a keyboard instrument.) The two instruments involved are the monochord and psaltery. The former, which led ultimately to the clavichord,[1] can be passed over here since it is the psaltery as forerunner of the harpsichord that draws our interest.

Known even in ancient times in the Far East and among the Egyptians, Assyrians, Babylonians, Hebrews, Greeks and Romans under names like *kin, tsche, sabbeka, nebel, magadis, sambyke* and *sambuca*, the psaltery was brought back to Europe probably by the Arabs or through the Crusades as the *qânûn* and *santîr*. From the ninth century we find it to have been used with ever increasing approval in secular circles as well as in churches, particularly, however, among the "minstrels et jongleurs." It appears in many medieval lists of musical instruments, and can frequently be seen in a large number of representations in manuscripts, paintings and sculptures (of King David, angelic concerts and the like).[2] The strings, originally in one set, later in several, are stretched between two pins or posts over a flat sound board, which is often provided with openings decorated with rosettes and shaped in the form of a triangle, rectangle, trapezoid or else rounded, often irregularly, and ultimately in a shape similar to that of a wing (compare the German

---

[1] See Hanns Neupert: *Das Clavichord. Geschichte und technische Betrachtung des "eigentlichen Claviers,"* 2nd edition (Kassel, 1956).

[2] A great many reproductions have been collected in Kinsky: *Geschichte der Musik in Bildern* (Leipzig, 1929).

term *Flügel*), which indeed is best suited to a course of strings varying in length. Later instruments have bridges on the sound board by which the string may be divided at will, usually in the proportion 2:3, so that on each string two tones a fifth apart are available. The production of tone was accomplished with the instrument lying on the knee or carried upright in the arm, hung up, or placed on a table, by the fingers or a plectrum, as is indicated by the derivation of the name psaltery from the Greek *psallein* (to pluck).

Even Athanasius Kircher in his *Musurgia* (1650) states that when played by a skilled hand, the psaltery is second to none. He also mentions that playing it requires great dexterity because the musician must use his hand as a damper while plucking the strings with two feather quills; this was necessary to prevent reverberation and the confusion of sound that results. The fact that the strings are excited by means of feather quills *(pennaceis stipulis)* points clearly to the close relationship between the psaltery and instruments of the harpsichord family. It should not go unmentioned that it is technically possible to strike the instrument with a blunt clobber and that this did indeed take place, in which case the instrument should properly be called dulcimer, from whose form in the 18th century the piano developed.

This technical identity despite the various manners of playing made it natural for the plucked psaltery to receive names which actually were more appropriate for the struck dulcimer; thus the term *cymbal,* from the Greek *tympanon* (a struck instrument), was applied to the psaltery, a plucked instrument. If we place *clavis* (key) in front of the name *cymbal,*[3] we arrive at the designation *clavicymbal* or as in German, borrowing and shortening the Italian *clavicembalo, cembalo.* Hence this name, originating as it does from compounds, quite accurately, symbolizes a technical development which has taken place since the 14th century.

The new arrangement by which the plucking of the strings is accomplished through striking keys is called a plectrum action. This plectrum

---

[3] The original word continues to exist in the name of the Hungarian *cimbalom,* which is a descendant of the dulcimer and is still in use, as is also the zither of the Alpine regions.

action is what the various members of this family of instruments with their many forms and names have in common; here I will mention as the most important only the harpsichord, the clavicyterium, the spinet and the virginal.

The keys, so essential in its construction, had already been generally used in the organ, which had been in existence for a considerable period of time. According to the description in Heron's *Pneumatica*, the water organ constructed by Ktesibios in Alexandria as early as the 3rd century B. C. used keyed levers to control the flow of air in the pipes. Then, as we know, the keyboard seems to have disappeared for about a thousand years to be replaced by movable sledges; it returned in connection with the increasing vogue of the organ in medieval Europe, particularly from the 11th century. At first one had to do with crude and heavy levers — the organ was quite literally struck — but the greatly favored small portative organ permitted more decorative forms and gradually there emerged out of the purely diatonic succession of pitches the chromatic keyboard with two rows of keys which is in use today. (The oldest example of this chromatic keyboard can be found in the organ of the cathedral at Halberstadt, built in 1361.)

The idea of combining a keyboard with a stringed instrument having produced the clavichord from the monochord, its application to the psaltery was a logical development. It is not now known just when the step to the psaltery with keys was taken, nor was it known to the writer of the earliest printed treatise on musical instruments, Sebastian Virdung (*Musica getuscht*, 1511).[4] He does, however substantiate this as the correct derivation of the harpsichord family in stating: "I believe, however, that the idea of making virginals arose from the psaltery now played by keys which were simple and provided with quill plectra; for although the instrument is made on a long board, like a clavichord, it has many more characteristics in common with the psaltery, seeing that each key has its own string, each string is higher than its neighbour in pitch, so that a lower string is always longer than its upper neighbour; the instrument takes the general shape of a triangle on account of the way the strings are cut and the gradually decreasing lengths of the strings."

---

[4] Facsimile reprint (Kassel, 1931).

The transitional type midway the psaltery-cymbal and the clavicymbal has been preserved in a pictorial representation in the basement of the church in Certosa near Pavia (built in 1472). Here, beneath the niches with their statues, is King David playing the psaltery. This instrument is thus described by Ambros:[5] "In form it is the well-known *istromento da porco* (shaped like the pig's head), a trapezoid formed by cutting off the top of an isoceles triangle by a crow section near the apex. David has the instrument lying in his lap, the base of the triangle towards him, its top facing out. The body of the instrument near the player's right hand is not closed but open and reveals within eight keys near one another which are related to eight strings running in the same direction. Under these a sound hole decorated with a rosette is to be seen. David operates the keys with his right hand while his left rests on the strings, apparently as a damper. It is well known that the greatest difficulty in playing the usual form of the psaltery consisted in having to damp the strings by the same hand which plucked them. The difficulty is solved here quite simply through the use of keys, which leave the left hand free to do the damping, while the right can easily perform even double stops. This practical and knowledgeable arrangement is a rather sure indication that Ambrogio Fossano or whoever made the statue did not portray an imaginary instrument; such a fantastic instrument would have turned out far more adventurously. The fortunate accident that an artist here made use of an instrument that he must have seen somewhere fills a substantial gap in the history of keyboard instruments."

In view of the lack of sources, additional information can be obtained only indirectly. For instance, poems[6] by the French poets Eustache Deschamps (1378) and Guillaume de Machaut (ca. 1370), the accounts of purchases made by Philipp the Brave, Duke of Burgundy (1385) and letters of John I, King of Aragon in the years 1387—1388, all mention

---

[5] Ambros: *Geschichte der Musik*, II (Breslau, 1864). Still another psaltery with keys, but one which is played upright like the portative organ, is represented on the altar of the church in Kefermark, Austria (built ca. 1480) and reproduced in Kinsky, *op. cit.*, 64.

[6] See Krebs: "Die besaiteten Klavierinstrumente bis zum Anfang des 17. Jahrhunderts," *Vierteljahrschrift für Musikwissenschaft*, VIII (1892); further, Kinkeldey: *Orgel und Klavier in der Musik des 16. Jahrhunderts* (Leipzig, 1910).

keyboard instruments with the plectrum action. On the other hand, Jean de Muris does not mention them at all in his *Musica speculativa*, written in 1323, so that we can place the time of their invention at the very latest around the midle of the 14th century.

These sources also mention an instrument which even today is somewhat legendary in character, the *eschequier*, *exaquier* or *eschaqueil* (in German, *Schachbrett*, chess board), "semblant d'orguens, qui sona ab cordis," that is, similar to an organ (probably because of the keyboard), but whose tone is produced by strings; its additional name *d'Engleterre* points to England as the country in which it was invented.[7]

Even though this statement conflicts with the fact that the great majority of the oldest extant instruments which can be dated are of Italian origin, it is not to be immediately discounted since we know that England produced the earliest independent keyboard music (the Robertsbridge Codex). Also in a German source, the *Minneregeln* of Eberhard Cersne in the year 1404, the *Schachbrett* is presented as corresponding, together with other instruments, to the English *eschaqueil*. Here we will leave open the question whether the German word is merely a translation (in which the unusual designation, chess board, for a musical instrument remains unexplained) or whether *Schach* comes from the Low German word *Schacht* (quill), as has been suggested by Curt Sachs (see his *The History of Musical Instruments*, New York, 1940, 337).

It is interesting to note that the *Minneregeln* also mention for the first time the clavicymbolum, so that around 1400 we can substantiate the existence of several different instruments all using the plectrum action. The differences between them lie in their various forms, as we will see later, while the aspect in common is the plectrum action, which we will now examine more closely.

---

[7] Recently H. G. Farmer in his *Studies in Oriental Musical Instruments* (London, 1931) reported on an Arabian stringed instrument mentioned by Al-Shaquandi (who died in 1231), the construction of which is as yet unknown.
The *scacachordum* or *scacrum* mentioned by J. C. de Gerson (1363–1429) may correspond to the German *Schachbrett*. An entirely different explanation for *echequier* is given by F. W. Galpin in the supplement to *Grove's Dictionary* (New York, 1944) in which he derives it from the French *échec* (stop or repulse) and thus considers the instrument as an early form of the piano (see the article "Chekker").

The function of plucking the string is carried out by the so-called jack (German, *Docke*[8] or *Springer*; Italian, *saltarello*; French, *sautereau*), a narrow piece of wood which rests loosely in an upright position on the end of the key-lever and which moves up when the key is depressed; one or two slots, the jack guides, make sure that the motion of the jack remains vertical. The process of falling back to its original position is usually facilitated by a piece of lead which is inserted into the jack, thus increasing the weight. At

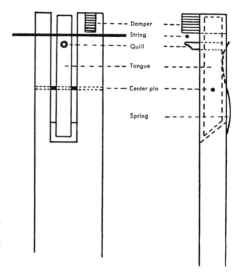

Fig. 1. *Diagram of a jack*

right angles to the upper part of the jack is a tongue in whose upper half is located the quill, which protrudes several millimeters. The tongue, which moves sideways in a slot in the jack, is controlled by a small spring of hog's bristle or metal located in the flat portion of the jack. The *modus operandi* is as follows. The quill, which normally rests immediately below the string, in moving up when the key is depressed plucks the string, causing it to vibrate and sound. On the return of the jack the tongue moves backwards, thus withdrawing the plectrum and avoiding a second contact between it and the string. Once the string has been passed, the spring forces the tongue back to its normal position, making the jack ready to function again. Damping the vibrating string is accomplished by one or two pieces of soft felt, cloth or leather mounted on the jack just above the plectrum, which come to rest upon the string when the jack is in its normal rest position.

The material used for the plectrum was originally taken from the quills of bird feathers. Let us in this respect hear from an old practising

---

[8] From the Italian, *tocchare* (to touch) and/or the Dutch, *tokkelen*.

musician, Johann Adlung, in his *Musica Mechanica Organoedi* of 1768: [9]
"One should consider further the feathers used to produce tone on all
harpsichords and instruments of this kind. Goose feathers would be too
soft and would not strike sharply enough. Occasionally I have used fish
bones, but these break and also are too stiff. Ostrich feathers are somewhat better, but they too are quite stiff and can easily break the strings.
Best are raven feathers, provided one can get the strongest ones. They
should be coated with olive oil so that they become tough and will not
easily snap or crack. Particular care should exercised that all the
quills are cut the same length, so that all will spring back at the
same rate; also that all are made equally stiff, since it is a great fault
when one key is harder to depress than another; and, further, that the
distance between the plectra and the strings is not too great, so that the
keys do not have to be depressed too far. Some people have tried to use
something more durable than feathers, which in time relax and become
useless in other ways, so that one is always repairing them, now here,
then there." According to this, the selection and treatment of the material
from which the plectrum is made is by no means a simple operation, and
it was desirable for the harpsichordist to be familiar with the quills used
in his instruments. For example, it has been said of J. S. Bach by his
biographer Forkel that he was skilled in this, just as he was in tuning
the instrument. It is also of importance that even in 1782 an English
catalogue offered plectra of crow and raven feathers as well as tuning
hammers. How different is the case with modern pianists and harpsichordists!

It is understandable that the search for materials more capable of
resistance went so far as to employ brass wire and small pieces of brass
shaped like blades for plectra, as was done by the organ builder Wiclef
or Wiegleb in Ansbach around 1724. [10] Possibly this metal plectrum is
much older, since Virdung mentions "nails, which pluck the strings."
This produced a stronger and brighter tone, which perhaps was felt to be
excessively sharp, quite apart from the fact that this manner of plucking

---

[9] Facsimile reprint (Kassel, 1931).
[10] Wiegleb was praised by Mizler and Adlung as the maker of a harpsichord with
built-in glockenspiel. In England, metal, ivory and tortoise shell and cork adapted to
be used as plectra were received by W. Barton in 1730, Roger Plenius in 1741 and
Hopkinson in 1785 respectively.

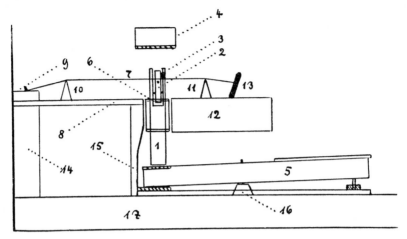

Fig. 2. The cross-section of a plectrum action.

1. Jack, 2. Tongue with plectrum, 3. Damper, 4. Jack rail, 5. Key, 6. Jack guide, 7. String, 8. Sound board, 9. Hitch pin, 10. Sound board bridge, 11. Wrest plank bridge, 12. Wrest plank, 13. Wrest pin (or turning pin), 14. Hitch pin block, 15. Cross block, 16. Balance rail, 17. Base.

had an adverse effect on the life the strings. Much more useful and of greater endurance was, on the other hand, the employment of small tongues of leather cut to the shape of quills; it is certain that such leather quills were known in the 16th century and were subsequently forgotten, then to be rediscovered around 1768 by the Parisian instrument builder Pascal Taskin (see his *Clavecin à peau de buffle*). This material naturally causes a slight difference in the tone color, which was often exploited in the larger instruments, in that one row of jacks was provided with leather quills, the other with feather quills. For these larger harpsichords with several sets of strings leather was more preferred in the 18th century. On the whole, leather produces a softer, more pure and round tone ("splendid like that of a double-bass," as Abt Vogler said) while feather quills sound sharper and brighter.

All this depends to a large extent upon how the material is prepared, so that, for example, in the *Musikalischer Almanach für Deutschland auf das Jahr 1782* leather is judged to be not only more durable but also to produce a "more masculine and brighter tone." On the other hand, Forkel in the *Musikalisch-kritische Bibliothek* (Gotha, 1778) refers to a *cembalo angelico* built in Rome which had plectra of leather covered with velvet

16

instead of the usual ones made of raven quills. "These pieces (of leather) sound as if softly touched by a sensitive finger and produce a tone combining the sound of a flute with that of a soft bell. In its fine quality of sound this instrument easily surpasses all others." Burney reports in Rees' *Cyclopedia* that ivory and other elastic substances were also tried, but with doubtful success: "what was gained in sweetness was lost in spirit." Philipp Emanuel Bach has also expressed himself on this matter:[10a] "A good harpsichord must have uniform quilling in addition to a good tone and the proper range. The tests of the quilling are the neat, facile execution of embellishments, and an equal, quick reaction of the key as the thumbnail sweeps over the entire manual with a light, uniform pressure. The action of the harpsichord must not be too light and effeminate; the keys must not fall too deep; the fingers must meet resistance from them and be raised again by the jacks."

Also of importance for the quality of tone are the strings themselves. Of the many substances that have been used, among which are sheep gut, copper, silver and even gold, iron, steel or brass are preferred. Virdung says in this connection: "The sound of brass strings is by nature coarse, while that of steel is fine so that if as many as four octaves or more are desired, one should use brass for the lower strings and steel for the upper." Adlung also expresses himself on this difference in tone quality, stating that the non-rusting "yellow" strings seem more durable and are preferred by him, although the "white" strings made of hardened steel wire "sound more charming and last longer," that is, do not break as frequently as the brass strings.

Experiments [11] have been made to determine the influence of thickness and length of the strings and particularly of the point of contact upon the quality of tone, since with instruments of the harpsichord family the strings must vibrate in specific proportional relationships. In contrast

---

[10a] Bach: *Essay on the True Art of Playing Keyboard Instruments*, transl. by William J. Mitchell (New York, 1949), 36–37. Subsequent quotations from this treatise are from this edition.
[11] Such experiments are mentioned, for example, in a letter from G. F. Duarte of Antwerp in 1648 (printed in Hipkins: *History of the Pianoforte*, London, 1896 and in Quirin van Blankenburg's *Elementa musica*, 1739). Covered strings were probably introduced in France by St. Colombe around 1675.

to the clavichord, where the string is divided into its several vibrating lengths only at the moment of contact, this division is pre-determined in the harpsichord and the plucking is all that is needed for the tone to be produced.

While the smaller members of the harpsichord family generally had one set of strings, the larger instruments had two, three or even four sets of strings. In instruments of this size the strings are tuned not only to the usual eight foot pitch (the term eight foot was originally used in conjunction with organ building, where the C pipe at one time had this length), but also the four and sixteen foot pitches, that is, an octave above and below normal pitch. The shorter four foot strings were installed beneath the eight foot set of strings and had their own bridges holding them on the sounding board; the long sixteen foot strings usually ran above the eight foot set. A set at the two foot pitch or at the fifth (mixture) was rare. Since each string requires its own jack, the number of rows (or registers) of jacks had to be increased in such instruments. To facilitate this, the jack guides, which we have already mentioned, were made capable of moving sideways, so that the inclusion or exclusion of whole rows of jacks could be accomplished at the player's desire. According to whether the quill was beneath the string, thus plucking it in passing, or whether it would pass by and miss the string, the register involved would either sound or not. At first these slides ran outside through the case of the instrument and could not be operated by the player while actually playing unless some further assistance was sought, similar to what was customary on organs. It was already an improvement when levers were introduced for this purpose, located inside the instrument (internal slides), eventually being made capable of manual operation in the form of stops which went through the case to the keyboard itself. Somewhat less frequent was the device of moving the register by pushing the keyboard backwards, making the keys control one or more registers of jacks. This method became important only for the coupling of manuals.

In the case of instruments of the harpsichord family there did exist a certain need for the incorporation of differing registers. The reason for this lies in the very nature of the plectrum action itself, which does not permit control over dynamics by varying the degree of force with

18

Fig. 3.
Cross-section
of a two manual
plectrum action
with two registers
of jacks

Action of a two manual harpsichord.

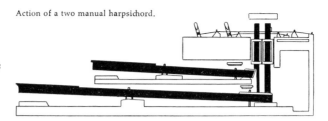

which the keys are struck, as can be done on the clavichord to a limited extent. This capacity has been developed to the full in the piano. If the working of the plectrum action is understood, one can see why this constant dynamic level comes about: whether the key is struck strongly or weakly does nothing to alter the fact that a vertically moving jack located a certain distance below a string plucks it with a plectrum. At the same time it cannot be denied that some small difference can be perceived when the keys are alternately struck strongly and weakly, as has been pointed out by, for example, Quantz in his *Lehrbuch der Musikpraxis* (1752) and Daniel Gottlob Türk in his *Klavierschule* (1802). Modern scientific measurements have demonstrated this phenomenon as well. The fact that a louder tone may be produced by striking the key harder is undoubtedly to be explained by the fact that a key which is depressed strongly makes the jack rise faster than usual and that thus there is greater amplitude in the vibrations, or greater volume of tone, since volume is proportional to the square of the amplitude. For practical purpose, however, it can be maintained that the sound of these older plectrum actions is capable of virtually no nuances by controlling how one strikes the keys.[12]

This shortcoming, which however turns out to be an advantage for the performance of a polyphonic composition whose parts are of equal importance, is counterbalanced by other advantageous aspects: relative to the physical characteristics of a plucked string, which, by the proper selection of the point where the plucking takes place, has a great many overtones,[13] a strong penetrating tone is produced which is not at all

---

[12] See on this subject, Dräger: "Anschlagsmöglichkeiten beim Cembalo," *Archiv für Musikforschung*, VI (1941).
[13] According to investigations by E. Meyer and Buchmann in *Die Klangspektren der Musikinstrumente* (Berlin, 1931), for the note c of a harpsichord (128 vibrations per

unsuited to accompanying singers, string and wind instruments, but rather reveals great ability to blend with them as well as to carry its own tone. Ideally the treble register has a bright "silvery" sound, which should not be unduly harsh, but must be "sweet"; Mattheson calls it "whispering and murmuring." The bass register should strive for a thundering, splendid, majestic, grave and pompous tone, which must however remain transparent, while the felt hammers of the piano sound dull and confused in this range. The advantageous features in the sound of the harpsichord have been enumerated by Couperin as *la précision*, exactness, in which every mistake is mercilessly exposed; *la netteté*, the joyful sweetness; *le brillant*, the radiant luster, the splendor.

Other physical characteristics of the harpsichord are closely related in principle to those now current in piano manufacture: the strings run from hitch pins, over a bridge on the sound board, to the nut and are finally wound around tuning pins (wrest pins) which are generally mounted in oak. Even in early times the sound board was usually made of well-aged fir, except when its more noble southern cousin, the cypress, was used. Beautifully carved rosettes of wood, metal or paper decorated the sound board and also provided for the passage of sound from the under side of the board. The reason for this is that these early instruments were built in box form, that is, with the underneath enclosed, since the board forming the bottom also served the same function as the modern inner laminated rim, the so-called back.

On this subject let us hear once more from Adlung: "The casing is occasionally made of a soft wood, but those made from hard woods will last longer. Painted and other forms of decoration are entirely at the discretion of the builder. The height of the case should be about half an ell (i. e., about 23 inches), but some are a little smaller, others larger.

---

second) thirty-three partials can be found, while a piano of the early 19th century has twenty-three partials, and a modern piano only fourteen. These figures silently confirm the unique quality of the harpsichord. Important in this connection is that when the string is plucked the partials set in at once and with full force so that the higher ones are relatively strong, while when a string is struck by a hammer, the fundamental and the lower partials are more predominant. A report on such physical investigations of the harpsichord has been made by Trendelenburg, Thienhaus and Franz: "Zur Klangwirkung von Klavichord, Cembalo und Flügel," *Akustische Zeitschrift* (1940).

When they are larger they take on a more serious and pompous appearance, but their tone is lovelier. The sides of the case may be made from either hard or soft wood and the bottom board is usually of fir, which strengthens the tone . . . The front has to be left open to provide room for the keyboard."

The keyboard consisted, as it indeed does today, of movable levers, each pivoting, almost centrally, on a balance rail and kept in position by guide pins; such a lever, when struck, causes the jack to rise. The keys were usually covered by a finger plate of ivory or ebony, although bone, box wood, pear wood or cedar were also used; in the more lavish instruments finger plates made of tortoise shell and silver can be found. For us it is particularly noteworthy that, in sharp contrast to our own practice, the sharps were frequently light in colour; for example, the sharps (our black keys) were covered with ivory, while the naturals (our white keys) would be covered with ebony; this custom originated in France, apparently to make the hands of the player more easily visible.

With regard to keyboard organization and range, all such instruments developed similarly to the organ, from which the keyboard did indeed originate. On the earliest pictorial representations we find a diatonic keyboard with two keys for B flat; and, more refined, a keyboard of thirty-eight containing five sharps in the octave from F to g", with the F♯ omitted. The bass range was extended from the F which existed as the lowest note through the Middle Ages down to 1500 to the note C. This extension was not accomplished as we might except by the addition of five keys, but rather by adding one key for the note C and making the D and E sharps (our black keys); the C♯ and D♯ were felt to be unnecessary. It was possible to use D and E in place of F♯ and G♯ since the latter could not be used as fundamental (root) tones due to the prevelant practice of untempered tuning. Such an arrangement was known as the "short octave." By means of it what appears as E-F-F♯-G-G♯-A actually sounds C-F-D-G-E-A. [14]

---

[14] Concerning these and other versions of the short octave, see Kinsky: "Kurze Oktaven auf besaiteten Tasteninstrumenten," *Zeitschrift für Musikwissenschaft*, II (1919), 65 f.

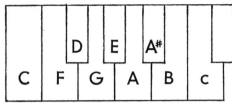

Fig. 4ᵃ. The Short Octave

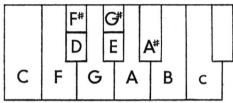

Fig. 4ᵇ. The Broken Octave

The actual size of the span of an octave in these older instruments was usually about $6^{1}/_{3}$ inches (16 cm.), hence somewhat small when compared with the roughly $6^{1}/_{2}$ inches (16.6 cm.) of the modern piano. The upper limit of the keyboard extended usually to c‴ or f‴, so that the total range would be four octaves and a fourth. As early as 1600 the short octave was adapted chromatically (a process known as *ravalement*). To reach the note G₁ a short octave was again employed, so that what appeared as B-C-C♯-D-D♯-E actually sounded G-C-A-D-B-E. Occasionally such shortened portions of the keyboard were filled in by dividing the upper keys in half, thus obtaining the missing half steps by broken (or split) keys; this procedure was also used to make enharmonic notes available. This rather contrived manner of construction was eventually abandoned and became indeed superfluous in respect to enharmonic tones when even tempered tuning was adopted in the 18th century. The final expansion of the keyboard to five full octaves, the so-called *grand ravalement*, took place around 1700, and the most common range is from F₁ to f‴. An instrument using this type of keyboard, with sixty-one keys, which in addition to the eight foot has both four and sixteen registers, has a total range of seven octaves, from F₂ to f‴‴, a range which is virtually never exceeded in the repertory of music proper to the instrument. This, however, is true only of the largest instruments, which were by no means numerous; the medium and smaller sized models often remained with a keyboard range of four octaves even in the 18th century.

Now a word on how the instruments were tuned: at the time a difference was made between *Kammerton* (chamber pitch) used for secular music

22

and *Chorton* (choral pitch) used for sacred music. Generally organs were pitched in the *Chorton*, while stringed instruments were tuned to the *Kammerton*. At the time of Michael Praetorius' *Syntagma musicum* (1618)[15] the difference between them comprised a whole tone; the *Chorton* was a whole tone lower to facilitate singing. Praetorius further states that somewhat earlier the difference between the two had been even greater and that in general a gradual tendency to raise pitch could be noticed, a trend that he did not welcome since stringed instruments go out of tune more easily when pitched higher. Particularly in the case of the clavicymbal lower tuning imparts "(as knowledgeable instrument builders are aware) a sweeter and more charming sound than if it were tuned to the *Kammerton*." Therefore, at the time there was no standard pitch in our sense (where A = 435, or more recently, 440 vibrations per second), although differences from country to country gradually became less and less, so that the English scholar Ellis could establish by means of testing pipes of various organs an A that varied only from 415 to 429 vibrations per second for this period. Briefly stated, one can consider that the music of the classical composers was played about a semitone lower than is customary now, which, along with other reasons, should provide an argument against raising pitch still more.

For tuning intervals among one another the Pythagorean perfect fifth method was standard at first, followed by the various systems of compromise temperament, whose merits varied considerably, designed to make modulation possible. Among these the mean-tone system of Arnold Schlick's *Spiegel der Orgelmacher und Organisten* (1511) with its pure thirds and somewhat diminished fifths maintained itself the longest and was superseded only at the beginning of the 18th century by equal temperament (Werckmeister in 1691[16] and Neidhard in 1706), which for the first time made possible that freedom in modulation, transposition

---

[15] Facsimile edition of part 2, "De organographia" (Kassel, 1929). For more information on this subject see Mendel, A.: "Pitch in the 16th and Early 17th Centuries," *Musical Quarterly*, XXIV (1948), 28; 199; 336; 575.
[16] Facsimile reprint of his *Orgelprobe* (Kassel, 1935).

and chromaticism which received its everlasting monument in J. S. Bach's *Wohltemperirte Clavier.* [17]

Thus we have outlined those basic aspects of construction and tone quality common to all members of the harpsichord family. In the next chapter we will examine the individual members of the family separately.

---

[17] For further information on temperament, see Dupont: *Geschichte der musikalischen Temperatur* (Kassel, 1935).

THE MEMBERS OF THE HARPSICHORD FAMILY

It was common in the Middle Ages to develop a whole family of instruments from one basic type and this is particularly true of the keyboard instruments with plectrum action. It is possible, however, to distinguish two principal groups of instruments from the numerous different models, many of which, to be sure, are mere duplications known under different names according to time and locality. We have the spinet and virginal on the one hand, the harpsichord on the other: a division simply between large and small instruments. The spinet and virginal resulted when a keyboard was added at the long side of a rectangular or trapezoid psaltery. The rectangular form, as given by Virdung in 1511 with the name virginal, is probably the earlier of the two. If, then, the corners of the case (which were quite superfluous to the operation of the instrument) are removed, a trapezoid, or more commonly, a five or six cornered form is the result, as can be seen in Praetorius' *Theatrum instrumentorum* of 1620.[18] Very often such irregularly shaped instruments are then enclosed in a larger casing, so that in appearance a box form results. Although earlier writers referred to this instrument in box form as a spinet, now we are inclined to look upon it as a virginal and to reserve the name spinet for irregularly shaped instruments. The diminutive term spinettino, therefore, is used for the very smallest model, whose shape is somewhat like that of a right-angled triangle.

Such designations, however, can not always be kept apart, since a great many changes have taken place and many of these terms have been used in a general way with reference to the harpsichord family. Even Praetorius found it necessary to write: "The large box-formed instruments as well as the smaller ones, both are called spinets in Italy without any differentiation. In England all such instruments, large as well as small, are called virginals. In France they are called *espinette*. In the Netherlands, *clavi-*

---

[18] Appendix to the *Syntagma musicum*, facsm. ed. (Kassel, 1929).

cymbal and even virginal. In Germany the instruments *vel peculiariter sic dictum* by species."

The following names also appear: *symphony* (whose meaning is not explained by Praetorius, but which according to a passage in Cochlaeus' *Tetrachordum musices* (Nürnberg, 1512) seems to refer to a clavichord with one set of strings; according to de Muris, it is the name given a hurdy gurdy in the later Middle Ages); and *buonaccordo*, according to Vincenzo Galilei's *Dialogo della musica antica e moderna* (Florence, 1581) apparently meant a small spinet, whose octave span was reduced so that children, with their small fingers, could use it for practising.

What I have already stated in conjunction with the term *schachbrett* holds also for the terms *spinet* and *virginal:* various shades of meaning exist for each. The simplest solution is perhaps most correct: it proceeds by good etymological methods and states that just as in the case of the *schachbrett*, *schach* is related to the plectrum, so *spina* refers to a thorn and *virga*[19] to a small piece of wood, the jack; in each case with reference to the most important aspect of the plectrum action, the material plucking the string.

There is, to be sure, some doubt as to the accuracy of this explanation, since the earliest source for either designation is from the 16th century, while the all-important plectrum action had long been known and could represent no peculiarity of the spinet. Or was reference made simply to the fact that, as already mentioned, in one instrument leather quills are used, while in the other, quills of thorn?[20] Also worthy of note is the possible derivation from the name of Giovanni Spinetti, a Venetian instrument builder active around 1500, who, according to the writer Banchieri (1609) invented the *forma longa quadrata*, the rectangular shaped casing for instruments of the harpsichord family.

---

[19] In the *Tractatus de canticis* of J. C. de Gerson, *virgula* is used in the sense of *plectrum*.

[20] Support for this is found in a passage in Scaliger's *Poetices*, lib. I (1561), where he states that instruments which in his youth were called *clavicimbalum* and *harpsichordum* are now known as *spineta* on account of the feather quills ("nunc ab illis mucronibus spinetam nominant").

Opinions on the interpretation of the term virginal vary considerably: the derivation from the "Virgin Queen" Elizabeth, whose love of music is well-known, must naturally be assigned to the realm of fable, in view of the fact that the term appeared much earlier, in Virdung (1511) as well as in an English proverb. In other respects the link to *virgo* (virgin) has much to recommend it, particularly since the earliest source to contain the term, the treatise by Paulirinus of Prague (around 1460) makes specific reference to it ("virginale dictum quod uti virgo dulcorat mitibus et suavissimis vocibus.") If, furthermore, we examine contemporary pictorial representations of musical performances, it will certainly appear striking that this instrument is almost always played by women (see pictures by Molenaer, Hooch, Terborch, Metsu, Steen, Dou, Netscher, Vermeer and others), while it is the lute or *viol da gamba* that is played by men. Early encyclopedias give the corresponding explanation, "because virgins and maidens play on them," so that the German term *Jungfernklavier* also appears justified.[21] Adlung's opinion in regard to the term virginal is that "the reason for this name being applied to these small instruments is their subtle tone," perhaps also the use of the four foot register. The term

---

[21] The relation between *virgo* and *virginale* and a specific connection between women and instruments of the harpsichord family is the object of a little study by the present writer published on the occasion of the *Internationaler Musikwissenschaftlicher Kongress*, held in Bamberg, 1953: "Die Frau und das Cembalo. Gedanken über das Jungfernklavier."
I am grateful to Professor Kuen, linguist at the University of Erlangen, for the following correction to my derivation of the term virginal:
"On the basis of linguistic reasons I can not believe that virginal in the meaning of keyboard instrument with small wooden plectra can be connected with *virga*, since this meaning could only be related as a virgin instrument to *virgo*. A derivation from *virga* would never have been *virginale* but *virgale*. Furthermore, there is no such diminutive as *virgina* from which *virginale* could have derived; rather, a keyboard instrument with wooden plectra would have been called *virgulare*, since the diminutive of *virga* is *virgula* and whenever the letter l appears in the root of a word, the endings —aris and —are occur, rather than —alis and —ale (see the singular and plural forms). "*Virginalis*, on the other hand, is a common Latin word and means, 'like a virgin, maidenly, pertaining to a virgin or maiden.' Hence, I believe that the earliest source for the term expresses its original meaning correctly: 'virginale dictum quod uti virgo dulcorat mitibus et suavissimis vocibus,' and that herefore the 'virgin' instrument is not so called because maidens and virgins are to play on it, but rather because its tone in comparison to other keyboard instruments in use at the time (portativ, positiv, regal) sounded maidenly, refined, delicate and sweet, opposed to their strong, masculine sounds."

virginal was most common in England, there often reffered to as "a paire of virgynalles," which, however, did not mean a pair in the sense of two, but was rather a plural form similar to *organa* for organ, *cymbala* for glockenspiel, etc., when a great many registers or manuals are contained in one instrument. By far the most frequent arrangement of spinets and virginals has one manual and one choir of strings with a range of something over four octaves, from C to c''', or sometimes from C to f''', in which case the lowest octave is a "short octave"; spinets with five octaves are of later origin and are rare. Due to the lack of varying registers, the sound tends to be somewhat monotonous. Its loudness is rather less than that of the regular harpsichord because of the space-saving sound board, in size somewhere between that of the clavichord and that of the harpsichord, as Mersenne states in his description of the spinet. The larger virginals are usually tuned to eight foot pitch, while the smaller instruments, as transposing instruments, might be tuned a fifth or an octave higher (four foot pitch). Such instruments are called *octavina* or *spinettino*. In the infrequent double virginals one can find eight and four foot stops combined when a spinettino is built into an enlarged case along with an eight foot instrument, to be drawn out and played, thus offering an enrichment of the available tone quality and an extension of the instruments's compass.

From the view point of construction, the essential aspect of all these instruments as opposed to the harpsichord was with the arrangement of the strings. The strings run diagonally to, or even overlap, the keyboard. The tuning pins (or wrest pins) are thus on the side of the case to the right of the player. Only in the octave transposing spinet, with its triangular case, is the wrest plank (or pin block) located along the front parallel to and somewhat above the keyboard, while the strings run sharply to the right. This arrangement is also used on the *spinetta traversa* of the 18th century, and, in spite of the shallowness of the interior, it permits the eight foot choir of strings to be arranged in the shape of a wing; in sound it resembles a harpsichord with one choir of strings. These instruments were built in Germany and England especially, countries which generally preferred the rectangular shape (as did the Netherlands), while in Italy the preference was for the irregular shape with five or six corners.

The oldest spinet to have come down to us was built in Italy and is the work of Alexander Pasii Mutinensis (i. e., from Modena), made in 1493. Other valuable examples are from 16th century Italy and include a spinet made by Annibale Rossi of Milan in 1577, ornamented with almost two thousand jewels, probably the most expensive keyboard instrument of all time. The Netherlands gained great importance in the building of virginals (i. e., *vierkante Clavisimbal*, rectangular harpsichord) and most of the production was carried on by a family of instrument builders, the Ruckers of Amsterdam, of whom we will have more to say later on. It was probably due to this Flemish influence that the building and playing of this instrument developed to the fullest in England. The art of virginal music at the turn of the 16th and 17th centuries represents a high point in English musical life, yet to be surpassed, in which the general public as well as the nobility, even the royal family itself, was actively engaged. It is no accident that the first printed music expressly for keyboard instruments with strings was engraved in England in 1611: *Parthenia or the Maydenhead of the first musicke that ever was printed for the Virginalls*, containing twenty-one compositions by Byrd, John Bull and Orlando Gibbons, notated on staffs of six lines. Of even greater importance among collections of keyboard music of the time are, among others, the manuscripts of *My Lady Neville's Book* (1591) and the *Fitzwilliam Virginal Book* (c. 1630). [22] Neither of these small members of the harpsichord family ever gained comparable importance outside England and remained instruments used in the home, while the principal role fell to the larger instrument in the family, the harpsichord, which we will take up now.

In chapter 39 of his *Instrumentenkunde*, Praetorius says this of the harpsichord: "The *clavicymbalum* is a long and narrow instrument often called *Flügel* (i. e., wing) because it is shaped in such a fashion. Some are called *Schweinskopf* (i. e. pig's head), because of the angular shape similar to the head of a wild boar. It has a strong, bright, very sweet sound and resonance, more than the other instruments of its family, on account of

---

[22] Here we should also mention the collections of keyboard music in tablature published by P. Attaignant in Paris around 1530, in which no distinction between works for organ and those for harpsichord is made, and which can only by divided according to whether they are sacred or secular.

its two-fold, three-fold or even four-fold sets of strings. I once saw one which had two choirs at the same (eight foot) pitch, one at the fifth another at the octave, which sounded sweet and magnificent together with one another."

I would like to expand somewhat this short explanation of its name, form, disposition and tone quality. The derivation of the term *clavicymbal* has already been discussed. *Gravecymbal* is either a dialectical change of letters, or from the Latin *gravis*, meaning large, heavy, an indication of the size and depth of the instrument. The largest instruments were also called *cembalone*. The shortening of the Italian word *clavicembalo* to *cembalo* was common chiefly in Germany and is universal there at the present time. In France the instrument is known as the *clavecin* and in England as the harpsichord. The German term *Kielflügel* not only refers to the plectrum action but also to the characteristic shape of the instrument (that of a wing). This similarity to the outward shape of a bird's wing is caused by the gradually decreasing length of the strings from the bass to the treble. In front, on the short side of the box (shaped like a right triangle with a rounded hypotenuse) is located the keyboard, in such a way that the keys run the same direction as the strings, while the wrest plank and the registers of jacks are at right angles to it. Such a manner of construction, when compared to the virginal and spinet, has the advantage that all the keys are of the same length, affording greater ease in determining the best point on the string for the plucking to take place, as well as making it easy to increase the length of the strings without causing the external appearance of the instrument to suffer unduly. This type of harpsichord, if it is not the original form, is at all events very old, as can be seen from the earliest pictorial representation of a harpsichord, in the Weimar *Wunderbuch* (ca. 1440), as well as from the description of a one manual harpsichord with a compass of thirty-five tones (B to a″) in the treatise by Henricus Arnaut of Zwolle, dated around 1440 (Paris, B.N., lat.7295).[23] In his *The History of Musical Instruments* (New York, 1940), Curt Sachs refers to a pictorial representation of a harpsichord that is even older, found in a miniature contained in the *Très belles heures* by the Duke of Berry (1409). The wing shape is con-

---

[23] Facsimile reproduction in G. le Cerf: *Instruments de musique du XV siècle* (Paris, 1932).

spicious by its absence in Virdung, who describes the *clavicymbalum* as a rectangular instrument whose strings run cross-wise, which is nothing but a reversal of the arrangement he gives as characteristic of the virginal. On the other hand, he is the first to furnish a woodcut of the *clavicyterium*, an instrument which we will now take up briefly. [24]

This instrument actually is a harpsichord whose body stands upright, a fact strikingly indicated by its name in the country where it is thought to have originated, Italy: *cembalo verticale*. Its action differs from that of the harpsichord only in that the up and down motion of the keys is changed to a back and forth motion of the jacks by means of an additional lever. The upright, space-saving form returned later in the *Giraffe* pianos with hammer action and thus this instrument may be regarded as an early forerunner of a type of piano popular today. A particularly interesting *clavicyterium* is owned by the Heyer Collection of the University of Leipzig: this instrument consists of two psalteries placed one on top of the other, so that the strings do not run vertically, as would be expected, but horizontally. This instrument is real proof of the fact that the harpsichord did indeed originate from the cymbal and psaltery. In his *Musurgia* (Rome, 1650), Athanasius Kircher maintains that the upright form was particularly used in Germany. Among its advantages he mentions the space-saving aspect, its decorative qualities and the possibility of using it as a harp as well as a harpsichord. However, in view of the small number of surviving instruments and descriptions, it seems that the *clavicyterium* was but rarely built and did not exert a great deal of influence, so that we can return to our discussion of the harpsichord itself.

The oldest example that has come down to us is a harpsichord of the year 1521, built by Hieronymous Bononiensis (of Bologna) in Rome, now owned by the South Kensington Museum in London. As already mentioned, most of the surviving instruments of the 16th century come from Italy, which must have been the center for the building of harpsichords at the time. In their arrangement and equipment these instruments show all the essential aspects of the later models. They are

---

[24] An early picture of an upright keyboard instrument with eight strings, which may be a *clavicyterium*, is contained in a Ms. from the Netherlands (Ghent, 15th century). See Van der Straeten: *La Musique aux Pays-Bas* (Bruxelles, 1885).

lavishly made, since even for instrument building all arts and skills were brought into play by men of the Renaissance and the Baroque, to please not only the ear by tone, but the eye by the appearance. Very often an instrument which is quite modest technically is housed in an especially elaborate casing, richly embellished with ornaments on its legs, grotesque figures and scrolls on the sides, designs using motives from mythology, history and nature inside, inscriptions by the builder on the jack rail or above the keyboard and the emblems of the owners, etc. Artists of the stature of Rubens, Boule, Watteau, Martin, Lorraine and Boucher placed their talents at the service of instrument makers, so that such a harpsichord would be a possession valuable to many generations. It was only from the 18th century that the decorations became simpler and more sober. Technical advances, however, provided a great difference between these instruments and their predecessors.

With regard to the harpsichord, attempts were soon made to do something about the unchanging quality of its tone, since there were no limits to its size or uses to which it might be put, as was the case with the virginal and spinet. The prototype for these attempts is easily found in the organ, not only in matters of performance and style of composition, but in regard to the close similarity of structure. Thus, different registers and manuals were applied to the harpsichord as they had been to the organ, to increase and enliven its potentialities both in tone quality and technically.

We have already seen that the registers, each with their own tone color, were activated by a set of jacks proper to each, controlled by stops. The use of the greater possibilities of tone color afforded in this fashion was considerably simplified by an arrangement of two or even three manuals, making it possible for the player to change tone color and dynamics, to emphasize certain parts, to produce an echo effect, or, by coupling the manuals, to play *volles Werk* or anything else characteristic of the "terrace dynamics," simply by quickly moving from one keyboard to another.

The simplest adaptation of a harpsichord with one set of strings and one manual was to provide it with a second row of jacks, which would immediately offer three possibilities for stops: one piano, one forte and together. Usually the second row of jacks would have its own set of strings, either in unison with the first (eight foot) or at the octave (four foot). The next step involves the arrangement of three sets of strings, where a division of the various rows of jacks between the manuals is advisable, since it offers more combinations. Finally, perfection is attained with four sets of strings, requiring two manuals, treated in such a way that either one manual can control most of the registers and would thus be a forte manual, or that the registers are equally divided between both manuals, so that a dynamic predominance of one (usually the lower) can be brought about only by a coupling arrangement.[25] C. Sachs gives us the following dates for the various stages of this development: 1514 for two registers with one manual; 1538 for the eight and four foot registers; 1576 for three sets of strings; 1582 for the four registers.

It is of interest to study the fashion in which the old harpsichord builders used the three basic aspects of the instrument, i. e., the number of sets of strings, the number of manuals and the various pitches (eight foot, four foot, etc.), since such an historical investigation provides information valuable for building harpsichords today, work which must rest on knowledge of this kind if it is to realize its basic principle of remaining true to the structure and style of the old instruments. To this end the writer has compiled a table[26] showing the relevant features of one hundred fortyeight instruments which he has either seen or of which he has read accurate descriptions.

Number of instruments	Sets of strings	Manuals			Registers
		1	2	3	
4	One	2			1 x 8'
		2			1 x 4'

[25] A particular type of register arrangement can be seen in the rare double *clavicymbel*. Here an octave spinet is placed in counjunction with a harpsichord (as was also true of the double virginal) by combining the two cases into a large four cornered box. The *spinettino*, with its own keyboard, enriched the tone of the harpsichord with its characteristically bright four foot pitch.
Ambros compares this instrument with a chapel built on to a cathedral or a corner tower on to a large castle.
[26] The writer is grateful for short descriptions and other data relating to a few old harpsichords in private ownership and in small, relatively unknown collections.

Number of instruments	Sets of strings	Manuals			Registers
		1	2	3	
70	Twofold	59	1		2 x 8'
		2			1 x 8', 1 x 4'
		8			2 x 4'
65	Threefold	13	37	4	2 x 8', 1 x 4'
		1	7	1	1 x 8' 1 x 4', 1 x 16'
		1	1		3 x 8'
8	Fourfold		5		2 x 8" 1 x 4', 1 x 16'
			1		2 x 8', 2 x 4'
			2		3 x 8', 1 x 4'
1	Fivefold		1		2 x 8', 1 x 4', 1 x 16', 1 x 2'
148		88	55	5	

In spite of the fact that the material from which this table was made is limited to a not extensive number of instruments, several conclusions can be drawn, which I will now outline.

A great majority of the instruments have two or three registers, divided about equally. Instruments with one or four registers are in the minority; in regard to the former, I would like to point out that only harpsichords, not spinets and virginals, are included here, to avoid giving a clear preponderance to instruments with one set of strings and one manual.[27]

---

[27] A substantiation of these findings is given in Adlung's *Anleitung zur musikalischen Gelahrtheit* (1758): "They (the harpsichords) seldom have one or four choirs of strings, but mostly two or three. Those with two are in eight foot pitch; those with three generally have two in eight and one in four; occasionally one of the eight

Even so, about two-thirds of the harpsichords surveyed have but one manual, about one—third of them have two, and only a few have three. The use of three manuals undoubtedly was an attempt to overcome the need for manually operated register stops by dividing the various registers among the manuals. The disposition of the three manual harpsichord was such that the lower manual controlled both eight foot registers, the middle one an eight and a four foot register, the upper only the four foot register. According to a remark in Marpurg's *Historisch-kritische Beyträge* (1757) this arrangement was used as follows: the lower manual for preludes and accompaniment, the middle one for *concertante* and solo playing, the upper for the echo effects common in the music of the period. Among the remaining possible arrangements, the following are found most frequently, hence they may be regarded as the most customary: the typical one manual disposition has two eight foot sets of strings and two rows of jacks which generally can be made to slide in or out. In the two manual disposition, the preferred arangement has two eight foot sets of strings and one four foot; the latter is controlled partly by the upper and partly by the lower manual. Instruments with this disposition made in England and the Netherlands often provide an eight foot set of strings with a second row of jacks (thus, three sets of strings and four rows of jacks).

Finally, one further harpsichord disposition with four sets of strings and two manuals has enjoyed some favor, even though in the past it was used but rarely: its attraction may be attributed to the fact that it is the same as that of the so-called *Bach-Flügel* of the National Collection of Instruments in Berlin. This harpsichord, whose maker is not known, simple in its external appearance, has a keyboard compass of five octaves (F1 to f'''), registers at eight and sixteen foot on the lower manual, a second at eight and one at four on the upper manual, a buff stop for the second eight foot register and manual coupling. Thus it is a prime example of an instrument whose resources are divided fairly equally between two manuals, although by means of coupling the lower can become dominant and *volles Werk* can be produced as well.

---

foot registers is replaced by a choir of covered strings at sixteen foot pitch. Those with four choirs of strings either have two at eight foot and two at four foot, or one of the latter is replaced by one at sixteen foot, either covered or plain."

The following registrations are available:

Without coupling	With coupling
8^1	$8^1 + 8^2$ $8^1 + 16 + 8^2$ $8^1 + 16 + 8^2 + 4$(Volles Werk)
8^2	$8^1 + 8^2$L $8^1 + 16 + 8^2$L $8^1 + 16 + 8^2$L$+ 4$
8^2L	$8^1 + 4$ $8^1 + 16 + 4$
16	$16 + 8^2$ $16 + 8^2 + 4$
4	$16 + 8^2$L $16 + 8^2$L$+4$
$8^1 + 16$	$16 + 4$ $8^1 + 8^2 + 4$
$8^2 + 4'$	$8^1 + 8^2$L$+4$
8^2L$+ 4$	L $=$ buff stop

If the convenient name Bach dispostiion[28] is given to this arrangement, the already mentioned disposition with two registers at eight foot and one at four can logically be referred to as the Ruckers disposition, since it is the usual one in instruments made by this firm, indeed it is often regarded as their own invention. This last cannot, however, be maintained any longer, since harpsichords built prior to their activity have the same disposition; but nonetheless the Ruckers family is of such importance in the building of harpsichords that we must turn our attention to them for a moment.[29]

Through the activity of the Ruckers the center of harpsichord building shifted from Italy to the North, first in Antwerp, where, even at the beginning of the 16th century, there were a great many builders of

---

[28] This designation, which has been in use for years, and not without good reason, has recently been questioned by F. Ernst: *Der Flügel J. S. Bachs* (Frankfurt, 1955) since the writer by analogy believes that the large *furnierte Clavecin* listed among the possessions left by Bach at his death probably was without the sixteen foot register and must have been according to the Ruckers disposition, or that of Couchet.

[29] Further information on the Ruckers family, particularly concerning extant instruments made by them, is given in the pioneering article in *Grove's Dictionary* by F. W. Galpin. A biographical study planned by G. Kinsky was unfortunately lost in manuscript during the war. Brief bits of information are given in A. M. Pols: *De Ruckers en de Klavierbouw in Vlaanderen* (Antwerp, 1942).

clavichords and harpsichords. Since 1575 "Hans Ruckaerts, clavisimbal-makerre" was among them as well as, in the years up to 1667, a number of other members of the same family, of whom Hans Ruckers the Older (born around 1550), who has already been mentioned, and his sons Hans the Younger (born in 1578) and Andreas (born in 1579) were the most famous. A way of identifying their instruments is the leaden rosette in the sound board, which represents an angel playing a harp, flanked by the initials HR, IR (for Hans the Younger, usually called Jean) and AR. The sound board on these instruments is always decorated with flower wreathes, birds, harlequins, etc., painted in light water colors. The underside of the lid often had wonderful paintings by Dutch artists, or else was covered with a type of paper printed with arabesques, which was developed in Antwerp at the time.

While the usual price of a Ruckers instrument was 20 pounds for a large harpsichord, 12 for a small one and 6 for the rectangular virginal, we know of an "IR" harpsichord, with a painting "Cupid and Psyche" by Rubens, which was sold to Charles I of England for 30 pounds. This can serve as proof of how good a name a builder of instruments can have had in foreign countries during his life time and the correspondence between Windebank, the State Secretary, and Gerbier, the painter active as an English agent connected with the purchase, is interesting in regard to the technical disposition of this instrument. Here they speak of a "dobbel staert stick," which was the term in the Netherlands for an instrument with two manuals, four registers, with the keyboards located on the short side (thus, like a wing in shape, but with the manuals on the shorter straight side). Particularly noteworthy is the announcement upon the arrival of the harpsichord that six or seven keys were missing.

We have thus touched upon an important characteristic of the two manual Ruckers harpsichords made in the first half of the 17th century: the manuals did not have the same range, but the upper manual, by means of a short octave, reached from C to c''', the lower similarly extended from C to f''', the space remaining in the bass range of the upper manual was taken up by a block of wood. In the treble, therefore, immediately beneath the key c''' of the upper manual was located the key f''' of the lower, which, however, struck a c''' string; in other words, the lower manual was pitched a fourth lower, an arrangement to make easier the transposition from *Chorton* to *Kammerton* that was customary at the time.[30] Later transposing harpsichords were built by making it possible to slide the keyboard sideways beneath the strings.[31] This arrangement, however, was considered to be more disturbing than its advantages warranted and it was obviated by increasing the compass of both manuals to a full four octaves (C—c³).

Further advantages in regard to technical matters as well as those pertaining to tone quality have been summarized by Hüllmandel in the *Encyclopédie méthodique* in the following way: "What distinguished these skilled instrument builders from all others, however, is overall superior quality, the fullness and well-balanced tone of their *clavecins*, achieved by careful and fortunately chosen proportions, by the most extreme care in the selection of wood for the sound board, by the great precision with which the various pieces of this wood were fitted together, so that its vibrations would be absolutely unimpeded, by a gradation in its thickness and density, related to the differing frequencies of the lower and higher tones."

Other developments that have been attributed to the Ruckers — that they invented the four foot register, that they were the first to use brass wire for the strings, that they were the first to have a four octave keyboard and two manuals — can, as we have seen, no longer be maintained, in view of the existence of earlier instruments possessing these features.

At the same time, however, it is not to be denied that these innovations came into general use only with Ruckers harpsichords. Thanks to their fine tone quality, these Ruckers instruments were in use until the end of

---

[30] The results of an investigation of this highly characteristic construction in an instrument of Andreas Ruckers in the Berlin State Collection is given in Alfred Berner: "Zum Klavierbau im 17. und 18. Jahrhundert," *Kongressbericht Lüneburg* (Kassel–Basel, 1950). A still more extensive discussion is given by Sibyl Marcuse: "Transposing Keyboards in Extant Flemish Harpsichords," *Musical Quarterly*, XXXVIII (N. Y. 1952), 414 f.

[31] Praetorius, *op. cit.*, mentions a transposing harpsichord with a keyboard that can slide up as far as seven steps of the scale; this instrument was owned by Karl Luyton, court organist in Prague and was built in Vienna around 1589. The so-called Prague *Mozartflügel*, a two manual harpsichord (lower manual with two eight foot registers, the upper with one four foot) made by Johann Heinrich Gräbner the Elder in Dresden in 1772, used by Mozart in Prague in 1787, has facilities for transposition by a semitone.

the 18th century, adapted to changing conditions by alterations and additions of various kinds. As an example, a large Ruckers instrument, once made by Andreas Ruckers in 1651, in mentioned in Händel's will. [32]

The influence of the Ruckers extends beyond the instruments they actually built through the work of their pupils, among whom Jean Couchet and Tabel are the most important. The former, a nephew of Jean Ruckers, is said to have added a second eight foot choir and to have transferred the four foot to the lower manual, thus making it a real forte manual since above it there was but one choir of strings, tuned to eight foot pitch. The latter injected new life into English harpsichord building, which in the 17th century, in the work of Keene, Haward and Hitchcock, had concerned itself principally with the smaller forms of the instrument: both of his pupils, the German Jakob Kirchmann and the Swiss Burkhard Tschudi (anglicized to Kirkman and Shudi), became very famous instrument builders. In contrast to the sweet tone of the Netherlands instruments, these English harpsichords strove for a powerful rounding of the tone by means of larger dimensions, by making the frame more substantial and by using stronger strings. Thus Burney, the English musician and writer, in his *The Present State of Music in Germany, the Netherlands and United Provinces* (vol. II) states: "... in general, the present harpsichords made here (i. e., Antwerp) after the Rucker (*sic*) model, are thin, feeble in tone, and much inferior to those of our best makers in England."

Among the two, Shudi won a leading position for himself through his collaboration with a young Scotsman, John Broadwood, who later, as his son-in-law, took over the business and became the largest manufacturer of strung keyboard instruments in England, a firm that is still in existence, the oldest of its kind. Händel, Frederick the Great, the Prince of Wales, Maria Theresa, Haydn — all of these have testified to the skill of the Shudi-Broadwood firm. The standard disposition of a Shudi harpsichord was as follows: two manuals, three sets of strings (two at eight foot, one at four) and four rows of jacks. [33] The fourth row of jacks, which

---

[32] The authenticity of this instrument has been confirmed by Carl Engels: *Musical Instruments* (London, 1908).

[33] The harpsichord built by Shudi for Handel belongs to the few instruments with two eight foot, one foor foot and one sixteen foot registers. For more information

was placed in front of the others, acted upon an eight foot set of strings already controlled by one of the other registers of jacks, but was arranged to strike it at a point near to the bridge, thus producing a tone quite like a lute or guitar; this was often also called the "cornet stop" or spinet. Otherwise this tone like that of a lute was produced by means of a lever that caused a bar covered with felt or cloth to be laid across the strings (buff stop). According to Praetorius such a harplike sound ("harfenie-rende Resonanz") was also brought about by "separate rows of brass hooks under the strings"; such an instrument he names *arpichordum*. Later, small pieces of leather pressed on served the same purpose. On Shudi's instruments, as well as on those of other English and French builders, there are two pedals to operate the various registers, along with the usual manual stops. The first mention of the use of pedals for registration is in Thomas Mace's *Musick's Monument* in reference to John Hayward of London around 1660, who placed four "little pummels of wood," pedals, but shaped like a "cubbord or box", now called the lyre, immediately below the keyboard, which caused the necessary sliding action. In the case of Shudi, one of the pedals operated the lute (or harp) stop, while the other provided means of introducing some variation into the unchanging dynamic level of the instrument, by operating the *Venetian Swell*, invented by him and patented in 1769. The idea behind this swell mechanism again goes back to organ construction, where in 1712 the firm of Jordans in London made an echo chamber with a movable front wall. Accordingly Shudi placed slides that could be opened and closed over the strings, somewhat like the modern Venetian blinds, thus making it possible to produce gradual crescendos and decrescendos at the will of the player.[34] His competitor Kirkman imitated the effect of this invention by causing the lid of the instrument to be raised and lowered, a device often found in early square instruments built in England and Germany.

---

on Tschudi and the Shudi-Broadwood firm, see the biography by W. Dale: *Tschudi, the Harpsichord Maker* (London, 1913) and the article "Broadwood" by the present writer in volume II of the encyclopedia *Die Musik in Geschichte und Gegenwart* (Kassel–Basel, 1952).

[34] A two manual Shudi-Broadwood harpsichord with the Venetian Swell cost 80 guineas; a one manual model with eight and four foot registers and the swell, 50 guineas; without the four foot register, 40 guineas; an eight foot instrument without the Swell, 30 guineas.

Among these efforts to alter the tone quality is the reintroduction of leather plectra on the jacks, as was done in the *clavecin à peau de buffle* made by the Frenchman Pascal Taskin in 1768, which has already been mentioned. Taskin and his teacher, Etienne Blanchet, belong to the famous group of French instrument builders whose ideal was a bright and delicate sound. Much of their work had to do with the enlarging and modernizing of instruments made in the Netherlands, but which were common in France. The *grand ravalement* is said to have first been accomplished by the Frenchman Nicolas Dumont. Finally, we should mention here Jean Marius, the builder of portable harpsichords that could be taken apart for travelling, the *clavecin brisé ou de voyage*, who is often thought of as a possible inventor of the hammer action used in the piano. The Italian Bartholomeo Cristofori, who now is generally recognized as the inventor of the hammer action, was one of the finest harpsichord builders in his country; among his predecessors we can list J. A. Baffo, Dominicus Pisaurensis and Giovanni Battista Giusti. In Germany, along with the firms of Hass in Hamburg and Gräbner in Dresden, that of Silbermann stands out; Gottfried Silbermann had close relations with Bach and with Frederick the Great; his nephew, Johann Heinrich Silbermann, was famous as a builder of organs and of harpsichords.[35] It is quite true that harpsichord building in Germany at this time in no way attained the proportions it enjoyed in the Netherlands and in England; it is probable that the confusion created by the Thirty Year's War in the 17th century had something to do with this, as well as the facts that the clavichord was particularly favored in Germany and that in the 18th century, with the intensive interest in music, Germany was the first country to take up the newly invented piano and to improve it.

So we come to the question of the harpsichord's part in musical life as a whole. The harpsichord and related instruments had to share the role of solo instrument from the 15th to the 18th centuries with the clavichord, even though, as previously indicated, in different countries there existed a real preference for one or the other. The literature for centuries had been intended as common to all keyboard instruments, that is, not only for

---

[35] Brief biographies of various harpsichord builders are furnished by Kinsky: *Katalog des musikhistorischen Museums von Wilhelm Heyer* (Cologne, 1910). On Cristofori, see the article by the present writer in *Die Musik in Geschichte und Gegenwart*, vol. II (Kassel–Basel, 1952).

clavichord and harpsichord, but also for organ and its smaller forms, such as the positive, portative and regal; in earlier periods it even included the lute and the theorboe. If we omit from consideration for the present the English virginal music of the 16th century and the French *clavecin* music of the 17th century, both of which were intended specifically for the harpsichord family, it can be said that differences between all these instruments in regard to technical, acoustical and idiomatic aspects were virtually neglected in the musical compositions. This should not be taken as a denial that certain characteristics may make a work seem more suited to a particular kind of instrument; but a conscious and intentional exploitation of the differing sound qualities of these instruments in a practical as well as a theoretical fashion did not occur until the 18th century. [36]

In his text book, *Versuch einer Anweisung, die Flöte traversière zu spielen,* Quantz states that each keyboard instrument "must be treated specially in a way suited to it alone" and we can find similar admonitions in the theoretical writings of Marpurg, Adlung, C. P. E. Bach *(Versuch über die wahre Art das Clavier zu spielen)* [37] and others. A considerably earlier observation of this sort is made by Girolamo Diruta in his *Transilvano* (1597), an instruction book written in dialogue form "sopra il vero modo di sonar organi ed istrumenti da penna," in which certain attributes of the harpsichord's tone are compared with that of the organ, as, for example, the necessity that the keys of the harpsichord be struck precisely on account of the action of the jacks and their quills. Musical effect is to be achieved by the quickness and skill of the hand, so that the keys are struck in rapid succession one after the other, but in so doing the melodic line is not to be disrupted, but rather should be embellished with trills and other ornamental decorations. Ornamentation was necessary in harpsichord playing because of the instrument's slight ability to sustain tone; the French developed this art more than any one else. The most important description of these embellishments is given by F. Couperin

---

[36] On this subject see Auerbach: *Die deutsche Klavichord-Kunst des 18. Jahrhunderts,* 2nd. ed. (Kassel—Basel, 1953), which gives many examples of music common to all keyboard instruments, various meanings for the term *clavier* and criteria for establishing the most suitable instrument to use in performances.

[37] A modern edition, ed. by W. Niemann (Leipzig, 1906). See also the English translation by W. J. Mitchell (New York, 1949).

in his *L'art de toucher le clavecin* (1761),[38] where the execution of each *agrément* is explained. This treatise is the first actual school of keyboard playing in the strict sense of the term, namely a work chiefly concerned with the development of technique pure and simple, in which the particular capacities of playing the harpsichord are gradually developed to a standard approaching virtuosity. Bach's little book of pieces for Friedemann[39] likewise contains a short "explanation of the different signs, which indicate that certain *manieren* are to be played"; such as the trill, mordent, cadenza, *accent*, etc. Furthermore, it was left to skill and musical sensibilities of each player to use still more elaborate ornamentations, to increase the general effect by employing diminutions, variations and the like. The exact use of the registers and manuals thus was left almost entirely up to the judgement of the player, who supposedly knew and appreciated what the disposition of his instrument made available to him. Works by composers of this period are virtually devoid of the dynamic markings which today are used to a degree that is almost excessive. Specific indications for registration exist only in a few compositions, as, for example, works by J. F. Dandrieu, Couperin's *Pièces croisées*, Handel's *Aylesford Pieces*, in which the use of manuals is indicated through the form of the notation on three or four staffs, as well as in Bach's *Italian Concerto*, in which the abbreviations *pia* and *for* clearly indicate the changes of manual. Very often a chance to alter registration is afforded merely by a short rest in one hand; in cases such as repetitions and echo effects, it was taken for granted.[40]

In any case, changes of registration on the older instruments could be made only to a limited extent on account of the awkwardness in the

[38] There is a new edition with German and English translations by Anna Linde (Leipzig, 1933).

[39] New ed. (first printed ed.) ed. H. Keller (Kassel, 1927). Facsm. reprint of Ms., ed. R. Kirkpatrick (New Haven, 1959).

[40] An interesting discussion of this subject can be found in Dolmetsch: *The Interpretation of the Music of the 17th and 18th Centuries* (London, 1915) and in Bodky: *Vortrag alter Klaviermusik* (Berlin, 1932). The technical data on the building of instruments discussed in the latter book have largely been superseded. As a guide to the study of older music, particularly of harpsichord playing from the 16th to the 18th centuries, as well as a reference book for performing musicians, we should mention Eta Harich-Schneider: *Die Kunst des Cembalospiels* (Kassel, 1939); there is a shortened English edition, *The Harpsichord. An Introduction to Technique, Style and the Historical Sources* (Kassel—St. Louis, 1954).

operation of the various pulls and levers, a fact which should not be forgotten when one performs music of this period. Quantz has very neatly indicated how a harpsichordist can bring variety into the sound of his instrument by the simplest of means:

"In the case of a harpsichord with one manual, a piano can be produced by striking the keys gently and by reducing the number of choirs of strings that are to sound; a mezzoforte by octave doubling in the bass; a forte likewise and also by having the left hand double tones of the chord; a fortissimo, however, by rapidly arpeggiating the chords from their lowest tones up and by doubling tones of the chord in the left hand, and by striking the keys more sharply. In the case of a harpsichord with two manuals one enjoys the advantage of using the upper manual for the pianissimo."

J. N. Forkel states the following in regard to J. S. Bach: [40a] "When he wished to express strong emotions, he did not do it, as many do, by striking the keys with great force, but by melodical and harmonical figures, that is, by the internal resources of the art. In this he certainly felt very justly. How can it be the expression of violent passion when a person so beats his instrument that, with all the hammering and rattling, you cannot hear any note distinctly, much less distinguish one from another."

Like the organ, the harpsichord was an instrument of terrace dynamics, of clearly articulated melodic lines, even though towards the ends of its period of greatest glory, the 18th century, a change in taste caused it to be equipped with swells, pedals and various other devices. Schubart gives a good characterization of the harpsichord: "Basically it has a simple outline, but it is finely drawn as a figure by Kneller or Chodowiecky, which consists entirely of plain lines with no shading at all. In playing this instrument one must first of all learn the art of playing cleanly, or, what amounts to the same thing, one must train one's hands in the art of musical drawing." Such a clear, sharply delineated sound, with all parts being equal, is quite favorable to the performance of polyphonic music, or fugues, and made it possible to have the various lines run quite

---

[40a] Translation by M. Stephenson, in David-Mendel: *The Bach Reader* (New York, 1945), 312.

close to one another in the bass register without having them obscured by excessive reverberation; this silvery tone was highly praised by musicians of the time, a fact neglected by those modern musicians who oppose the use of the harpsichord. The mere fact of the rise of the keyboard concerto itself, whether a solo concerto, or with orchestral accompaniment, can be taken as proof of the great esteem in which the harpsichord was held. In playing the harpsichord everything depends more upon the player than upon the instrument itself, as Quantz rightly remarks, and there is no doubt that a virtuoso command of the harpsichord requires more skill than is needed for similar ability on the piano. As a good means of developing skill in playing the harpsichord, theorists from Virdung to C. P. E. Bach often mention the clavichord, which provides us with yet another proof of the close relationship that existed between these two contemporary instruments, a relationship which formed our original point of departure.

Both harpsichord and clavichord possess in common something quite essential for the student, that is, the string can be felt directly through the keys: the plectrum action allows the player to feel the tension and resistance of the strings, lets him feel the proper amount of pressure needed and then finally to apply it and overcome the strings' resistance. This immediate relation to the vibrating string, which lasts until the string is actually set in vibration, exists also in the clavichord, except that there it is maintained during the string's actual period of vibration, until its cessation. In contrast to these is the hammer action of the piano, in which an elaborate system of levers stands between the player's hand and the sounding strings. From this fact alone we can discern a close bond between the harpsichord and the clavichord.

A particular task was assigned to the harpsichord over all other keyboard instruments except the organ, and this was its not unimportant use as an accompanying and continuo (thorough bass) instrument. The clavichord, its expressive tone notwithstanding, could not be used since its volume of tone was far too weak, while the stronger harpsichord sound, which blended well with other instruments, provided a tonal and rhythmic support. With the rise of the *stilo nuovo* in the 17th century, the harpsichord won for itself the task of performing the *basso continuo*; this applies to large instruments as well as to the smaller models with one set of strings. Other instruments, like the lute, also performed the *basso continuo*, but a serious challenge to the harpsichord was presented only by the organ in the field of church music, where it was difficult for the comparatively secular harpsichord to find a place for itself. In this capacity the harpsichord was predominant in connection with opera, orchestra music (suites and concerti grossi) and in trio sonatas, and the player had beyond the proper performance of the figured bass the duty of supplying a richly improvised accompaniment. C. P. E. Bach states in regard to the continuo player, that he must play "now with many, now with fewer parts, now in strict accordance with the harmony, now in galant style." As early as 1607 two harpsichords were part of Monteverdi's orchestra, and were assigned individual roles in the accompaniment of recitatives and arias. The director of the orchestra sat at the first harpsichord *(maestro al cembalo)* and his importance exceeded that of the cantor and organist, while the second instrument served as a harmonic filler and supplemented in a general way the sound of the orchestra. For an ensemble consisting of eight violins, two violas, three 'celli, one bass and wind instruments in pairs, Quantz recommends the use of one harpsichord; for a larger ensemble, consisting of twelve violins, three violas, four 'celli, two basses, four flutes, two oboes and three bassoons he recommends two harpsichords and one theorboe. Here it must be remembered that at this time string instruments had less volume than they do today. The sound of the harpsichord did not stand out as much as does, for example, that of the modern piano. Even so, it was considered quite indispensable, as we can see from the famous theorist, Mattheson, who states in his *Das neueröffnete Orchester* (1713): "In its *université* the harpsichord is an excellent accompanying instrument and is virtually indispensable to church, theatrical and chamber music; it is a wonder that here (Hamburg) they still cling to the snarling and disgusting sound of the regal in the churches, since the murmuring and whispering of the harpsichord, of which two can be used if necessary, produces a far more beautiful effect with a chorus. In French music the harpsichord is not felt to be quite so necessary and a bass violin or something similar is commonly employed as a fundamental instrument; however, it sounds so empty and naked that a connoisseur feels ashamed and one who does not really understand music has no idea what is missing."

This view is supported by Quantz, who states: "My view is that the harpsichord should be used at all musical performances, the larger as well as the smaller," and by C. P. E. Bach: "No piece can be well performed without some form of keyboard accompaniment. Even in heavily scored works, such as opera performed out of doors, where no one would think that the harpsichord could be heard, its absence can certainly be felt. And from a position above the performers all its tones are clearly perceptible. I base these observations on experiences which may be duplicated by anyone." [40b]

Characteristic of the close link with the orchestra it was that the harpsichord was placed in the center of the ensemble, as is proved by pictorial representations of performances of the time. [41] It maintained its accompanying role in operas, cantatas and oratorios for quite a long time, even into the early 19th century, while as a solo instrument it gradually fell out of use in the closing decades of the 18th century and ultimately was replaced by the piano, which surpassed the harpsichord that "either could not render any colour at all, or else expressed it through stops in terms of the strongest possible contrasts."

It is clear from this description that the harpsichord was not the victim of technical advances in the construction of instruments, but rather of one of the greatest changes in musical style in the whole history of music. Technically the 18th century piano was no better than the harpsichord, with which it had only the keyboard in common. The piano was something quite different and was better suited to the demands of a new musical idea and a new type of dynamics, and thus it carried the day, just as the violin replaced the softer viols and gambas, as the transverse flute replaced the recorder. The harpsichord builders of the time were certainly by no means lacking in ingenuity, since apart from the usual added registers there are yet a number of rather adventurous efforts, mostly of a fly by night character, but which yet deserve a little attention. The central purpose behind all such attempts was to increase the period of the strings' vibration and to gain direct control over the volume of

---

[40b] Bach, op. cit. (transl. W. J. Mitchell), 173.
[41] An extensive treatment of instrumentation, etc., is given in Haas: Aufführungspraxis der Musik (in Bücken, ed · Handbuch der Musikwissenschaft, VIII, Potsdam, 1931).

tone, all problems that exist even today and in the solution of which electronic devices of various kinds are now being employed.

The oldest recorded attempt of this kind is the *Geigenclavicymbel* built around 1610 by Hans Hayden of Nürnberg. It had five or six wheels whose rims were covered with parchment and painted with rosin which were set in motion by a foot pedal. The strings of steel and brass, which ran across bow-shaped bridges, were forced against the wheels when the keys were depressed and were set in vibration as if by the stroke of a bow as long as the key was held down. This manner of operation led its inventor to prefer it to the usual harpsichord: "the tone can be sustained as long as one wishes." Although this invention aroused much admiration among contemporaries, it did not gain any general acceptance, due to the fact that at the time no need was felt for expressiveness of this kind in musical performances. Similar instruments appeared quite frequently, such as the one built by the Spaniard Truchado in 1625, the *Arched Viall* in England around 1664, the instrument built by Cuisinié in Paris (1708), characteristically called a *clavecinvielle*. The last two of the above mentioned instruments recall the prototype of the medieval *vielle* which employed a rotating wheel instead of a bow (the hurdy gurdy). When strings similar to those of the *viola da gamba* were employed in 1709 by Gleichmann, an organist at Ilmenau, the name *Klaviergambe* was used. An improved manner of construction was worked out by Le Voir of Paris in 1742 and, particularly, by Hohlfeld of Berlin in 1754, in his *Bogenflügel*, which was famous at the time; this instrument substituted for the violin bow an endless belt of horse hair which ran along under the strings and stroked them when the keys were depressed. Strings made of cat gut were used by the English builder Roger Plenius in 1741, who claimed his instrument to be capable of imitating the sound of the violin, violoncello, double bass and the organ as well, adding the further advantage that it "never goes out of tune," thus making use of some permanent means of maintaining the tension of the strings, thereby obviating an ancient weakness of the harpsichord.

While such friction instruments are rather far removed from their point of departure, the harpsichord, others, like the *Theorbenharfe*, *Lautenclavicymbel* and *Klavierharfe*, are much closer to it, since in each the strings are plucked. The *Theorbenflügel*, invented by J. C. Fleischer of

Hamburg in 1718, employed for the sixteen foot register strings made of cat gut and his *Lautenklavier* used them in its eight foot register (cat gut strings had been known since Virdung). The latter is especially interesting since it has a connection with the work of J. S. Bach; according to Adlung and Spitta, around 1740 Bach had Zacharias Hildebrand, organ builder in Leipzig, build such an instrument according to his own specifications, with two sets of cat gut strings of eight foot pitch, and a four foot register with brass strings; apparently he considered this a satisfactory means of performing his lute compositions on a keyboard instrument. It was just such a *Lautenclavicymbel* which in the hands of a skilled player, could deceive even professional lutenists. J. N. Bach of Jena had particular skill in the building of such instruments, making them even with three manuals and registers of jacks whose plectra were so arranged that each plucked the strings with greater force. Finally, the *Klavierharfe*, which also belongs here, represented an attempt to combine an ordinary harp and a keyboard operating a plectrum action making use of small curved hooks. Although described by Mersenne as early as the 17th century, it became somewhat more widely known after 1814 through the efforts of J. C. Dietz in Paris, without, however, attaining much significance.

The same fate awaited all other attempts to make the harpsichord sound like other instruments by countless new register stops and new manners of playing. Reichardt pronounces the harsh but proper verdict on all such efforts: "All these newly designed keyboard instruments using six to twelve different stops are strictly patchwork and suited only for children's games." It is only for the sake of completeness that I mention here the *Denis d'or* made by Prokop Divis of Bohemia in 1730, which had seven hundred and ninety strings and one hundred and thirty different register changes to imitate all the string and wind instruments, or the *clavecin harmonieuse et céleste* made by Virbès in France, which somewhat modestly restricted itself to imitating the sound of but fourteen instruments. Such attempts provided the groundwork for later mechanical instruments, orchestrions, etc. Mechanical instruments with plectrum action are rarely found as early as the 17th century in England, the Netherlands and Germany.[42]

---

[42] On this subject, see Protz: *Mechanische Musikinstrumente* (Kassel, 1939). Samuel Bidermann of Augsburg was especially famous. In C. Weigel's *Abbildung der*

Forerunners of contemporary quarter tone pianos and instruments capable of so-called pure diatonic tuning exist as early as the 16th century in experimental instruments constructed by Nicolo Vicentino, Zarlino, Nigetti, Mersenne and others under such names as *arcicembalo*, *clavicymbalum universale*, *cembalo omnisono*, *cembalo enarmonico*, etc. They contain diatonic, chromatic and enharmonic steps in each octave, using several manuals and broken keys for the smaller steps. They became nothing but scientific experiments upon the adoption of even tempered tuning.

Greater practical significance was reached in the technical combination of the harpsichord with other types of instruments. The *claviorganum* existed for a long period of time, since it is mentioned in the *Tractatus de musica* by Paulirinus of Prague in 1460 and one was owned by a Spanish noble in 1480; according to other reports it seems to have been fairly widespread. Its construction is described by Praetorius: "the *claviorganum* is a harpsichord, or similar instrument, which along with the strings has a group of pipes, like those of a positive, mixed in; in appearance it looks exactly like an ordinary harpsichord or symphonium, except that in some models the bellows are located on the back side, while in others they are placed inside the case." Later the clavichord and even the piano were similarly provided with pipes.

Still another relation to the construction of the organ can be seen in the *clavicymbelpedale*, harpsichords with pedals like those of organs, which are either connected directly to the bass keys of the instrument, or else have their own set of strings and jacks over a two octave compass at sixteen foot pitch, upon which the harpsichord itself was placed. The invention of the pedal harpsichord is frequently attributed to Bernhard, a German organist active in Venice around 1470 on the basis of a passage in the works of Sabellicus, an historian who died in 1506: Bernhard fastened loops of rope to the organ keys, so that they could be played by the feet. The practice probably goes back to Louis van Valbecke of Brabant, who died in 1318. Pedal clavichords, mentioned in treatises in

---

gemeinnützlichen Hauptstände (Regensburg, 1698) reference is made to "spinets, both simple and elaborate which by themselves through special arrangements play certain songs, dances and harmonies; such instruments are made in Augsburg and are concealed in pin cushions, desks, cabinets and all other pieces of furniture; they have spread out over the whole world."

the second half of the 15th century and also by Virdung in 1511, and pedal harpsichords were used by organists as instruments on which to practice at home. Forkel states of Bach, that for improvisation he liked to use "two manuals and pedal, or a two manual instrument with pedals." Like Schweitzer he refers the Passacaglia and the six trio sonatas to such an instrument; the third part of the *Clavierübung* is also suited to it.[43] As the finest *untergesetztes Klavicymbelpedal* Adlung mentions an instrument with two eight foot registers and one sixteen foot, owned by Mayor Vogel of Weimar. As a curious combination of harpsichord, clavichord and piano there is the *Tangentenflügel*, invented by Späth of Regensburg around 1750 and later built in association with his step-son, C. F. Schmahl. In this instrument little pieces of wood mounted in guide slots functioned as tangents by striking the strings; its lack of tonal expressiveness denied it any lasting success.[44]

A definite sign of the diminishing importance of the harpsichord can be seen in its combination with the piano. The most significant examples of this coupling of two instruments so different in tone quality, in which the harpsichord part was to provide the articulation and the silvery, incisive sound, while the piano the dynamic coloring, are known as *Polytoni-clavichordium* and *Saitenharmonika*. It is characteristic that both types of instruments were built by those firms that were leaders in building "progressive" instruments, that is, Johann Andreas Stein of Augsburg[45] and Sebastian Erard of Paris, both of whose inventions in regard to the hammer action helped greatly to seal the fate of the harpsichord. The original notion of the hammer action occurred almost fifty years before the great change in musical style. Many decades were needed for its technical development, until at the end of the century a change in musical sensibility made the new instrument the successor of the harpsichord.

---

[43] On this see Kinsky: "Pedalklavier oder Orgel bei Bach?," *Acta musicologica*, VIII (1936), 158 f., which, in addition to the description given by Adlung, refers to the even older account of Nicolas Douwes: *Grondig ondersoek van de toonen der musijk* (Faneker, 1699).

[44] See also Hermann: *Die Regensburger Klavierbauer Späth und Schmahl und ihre Tangentenflügel* (Erlangen, 1928).

[45] For further information on the origin and technique of the *Polytoniclavichordium* (1758) and the *Saitenharmonika* (1788), see Hertz: *Joh. And. Stein. Ein Beitrag zur Geschichte des Klavierbaus* (Wolfenbüttel, 1937). Further, K. A. Fischer: "Joh. And. Stein, der Augsburger Orgel- und Klavierbauer," *Zeitschrift des historischen Vereins für Schwaben und Neuburg* (Augsburg, 1932).

I will conclude this discussion of the early harpsichord with a list of leading composers of music for the instrument, most of whom were performers as well as composers. In accordance with the character of this booklet I will limit myself to a mere list in the form of a table and for the rest will mention the most important books on this subject, such as Seiffert-Weitzmann: *Geschichte der Klaviermusik* (Leipzig, 1899); Westerby: *The History of Pianoforte Music* (London, 1924); Schünemann: *Geschichte der Klaviermusik* (Berlin, 1940); Georgii: *Klaviermusik* (Berlin—Zürich, 1942).

Germany

Konrad Paumann	1410—1473
Elias Nikolas Ammerbach	1530—1597
Hans Leo Haßler	1564—1612
Heinrich Schütz	1585—1672
Samuel Scheidt	1587—1654
Johann Jakob Froberger	1616—1667
Johann Adam Reinken	1623—1722
Johann Kaspar Kerrl	1627—1693
Johann Dietrich Buxtehude	1637—1707
Georg Muffat	1645—1704
Johann Kaspar Fischer	1650—1746
Johann Krieger	1651—1735
Johann Pachelbel	1653—1706
Johann Kuhnau	1660—1722
Georg Böhm	1661—1733
Franz Xaver Murschhauser	1663—1738
Johann Mattheson	1681—1764
Georg Philipp Telemann	1681—1767
Georg Friedrich Händel	1685—1759
Johann Sebastian Bach	1685—1750
Gottlieb Muffat	1690—1770
Philipp Emanuel Bach	1714—1788
Friedrich Wilhelm Marpurg	1718—1795

England and the Netherlands

Thomas Tallis	1505—1585
William Byrd	1543—1623
Thomas Morley	1557—1603
Peter Philips	1560—1633
Jan Pieters Sweelinck	1562—1621
John Bull	1563—1628
Giles Farnaby	1565—1598
Orlando Gibbons	1583—1625
Matthew Locke	1632—1677
John Blow	1648—1708
Henry Purcell	1658—1695
Thomas Arne	1710—1778

Spain and Portugal

Felix Antonio de Cabezon	1510—1566
Manuel Rodrigues Coelho	1583—1623
Carlos de Seixas	1704—1742
Antonio Soler	1729—1783

France

André de Chambonnières	1602—1672
Jean Henri d'Anglebert	1628—1691
Antoine le Bègue	1630—1702
François Couperin	1668—1733
Louis Marchand	1669—1732
Jean Philippe Rameau	1683—1764
Jean François Dandrieu	1684—1740
Claude Daquin	1694—1772

Italy

Adrian Willaert	1490—1562
Jacques Buus	† 1565
Andrea Gabrieli	1510—1586

Claudio Merulo	1533—1604
Luzzasco Luzzaschi	1545—1607
Giovanni Gabrieli	1557—1612
Adriano Banchieri	1567—1634
Girolamo Frescobaldi	1583—1643
Bernardo Pasquini	1637—1710
Francesco Durante	1684—1756
Domenico Scarlatti	1685—1757
Nicolo Antonio Porpora	1686—1766
Giovanni Battista Martini	1706—1784
Baldassare Galuppi	1706—1785
Pietro Domenico Paradisi	1710—1792

MODERN HARPSICHORD BUILDING

The harpsichord was buried in oblivion up to the end of the 19th century. Even so, works written by great composers for the instrument were given an new lease of life once the way had been opened by the performance of Bach's St. Matthew Passion in 1829 and by the work of Chrysander, Fétis, Spitta and others, especially in the various *Denkmäler* publications. But in place of the harpsichord there was the piano, whose originally bright and rather thin sound later became that of the mighty concert grand. No one had any reservations about how the sound of the music had been altered by such a modern adaption. Only with further progress in historical knowledge and the development of aesthetic sensibilities did it come to be recognized that research and republication could only accomplish half of the task and that a true revitalization of the music was inextricably bound up with the use of the instruments for which it was originally composed.

The first organization to undertake this actively was the *Société des anciens instruments* [46] founded in Paris in 1889. It is for this reason that a beginning in the modern construction of harpsichords was made in Paris around 1888, when the two piano manufacturers, Erard and Pleyel, began building modern harpsichords with two manuals. The Pleyel harpsichord found a great exponent in Wanda Landowska, who has done work of permanent value in the reestablishment of the instrument. [47]

---

[46] The corresponding organization in Germany was the *Deutsche Vereinigung für alte Musik*, founded in Munich (1905). Even in previous decades, however, isolated performances employing old harpsichords in sufficiently good condition took place in England as well as in France and Germany (for example, by Moscheles, von Pauer, Diémer and Buchmayer). Since then several such organizations have come into existence in various countries: *Musica antiqua* (Amsterdam), *Pro musica antiqua* (Bruxelles); *Society of Ancient Instruments* (Philadelphia); and, most recently, the *New York Pro musica antiqua*. Many universities and schools of music maintain similar groups.

[47] In a highly individual way Landowska has given her views on the proper rendition of early music in her book, *La Musique ancienne* (Paris, 1908; English ed., *Music of the Past*, trans. W. A. Bradley, London, 1926) and in the article "Le clavecin chez

What a few decades ago had been nothing but the ideal of a few enthusiasts and seemingly the privilege of musicological research seminars began to spread more and more, so that it is possible to speak of a harpsichord revival (since 1920) which merged with similar movements encouraging the cultivation of music by young people and reforms of music in the schools. There have even been important contemporary works composed for the harpsichord, such as compositions by Heinz Bartl, Jürg Baur, Siegfried Borries, Willy Burkhard, Castelnuovo-Tedesco, J. Nepomuk David, Heinz Degen, Hugo Distler, Manuel de Falla, Dante Fiorillo, Wolfgang Fortner, Hermann Fuchs, Werner Haentjes, Lou Harrison, Werner Henze, Hugo Hermann, Karl Höller, Wolfgang Jacobi, Heinrich Kaminski, Ellis Kohs, Hubert Lamb, Konrad Lechner, Ernst Levy, Gerhard Maahs, Wilhelm Maler, McBride, Frank Martin, Peter Mieg, Siegfried Walther Müller, Charles Naginski, Robert Oboussier, Emil Peeters, Walter Piston, Francis Poulenc, Mel Powell, Goffredo Petrazzi, Edmund Rubbra, Karl Schäfer, Kurt Thomas, Virgil Thomson, Hermann Wolfgang von Waltershausen and Friedrich Zipp, among others. Well-known performers and teachers have also participated.

Important contributing factors are, on the one hand, the general historically minded attitude of our time, and, on the other, a change from modern concert activity with its emphasis upon virtuosity to making music in common, the *collegium musicum*, the small music group. Under these circumstances the modern concert grand piano is not always looked upon as an improvement on the harpsichord, but only as an instrument with an entirely different quality of sound. Each epoch has its own characteristic ideal ("Klangideal") and creates the instruments necessary for its realization.

The fact that the harpsichord is now being revived in performances of keyboard music written up to end of the 18th century is nothing more than a demand that the artistic intent of these composers be respected in the selection of the instrumental medium. Let us look upon the problem from the other side, as has been done by Oskar Fleischer in an article, "Das Bach'sche Clavicymbal und seine Neukonstruktion" (1899): "A

Bach." For other important articles, see the *Bach-Jahrbücher* (published by the *Neue Bachgesellschaft*), especially for the years 1908–1910 and the *Jahrbuch der Musikbibliothek Peters* (Leipzig, 1903).

contemporary composer would probably protest if one were to perform his rhapsodies, polonaises and fantasias on a harmonium—or what in principle is not really different—on a harpsichord, thus making a ludicrous parody. He would complain loudly and with justice at such a mistreatment of his artistic creations. Yet he remains silent when masters long dead, who can no longer protest, are treated in exactly the same way and he is content to trample their rights into the dust at the first opportunity."

The harpsichord is first and foremost the instrument of contrapuntal lines, of clarity, of sharply differentiated tone qualities in different registers, as opposed to the romantic and emotional use of dynamics and emphasis upon sheer volume of tone characteristic of the piano. There is no intent here to question the significance and value of the piano—an instrument with which I have as much professionally to do as I have with the harpsichord—nor to deny it as a medium for the performance of early music whenever skilled arrangers and responsible performers can attain effects similar to those characteristic of the harpsichord. On the other hand, an historical and aesthetic consciousness should be developed, which sees the ideal only in a performance using the proper and authentic instrumental medium. There is no question of doing away with the piano, but rather of destroying its exclusive grip [47a] and making the audience aware of the difference between the two instruments. Opponents of this point out that many of the greatest musicians of former centuries envisioned the modern piano, which they would have warmly greeted had it appeared in their lifetimes. [48] This, however, cannot alter the historical

---

[47a] See Ludwig Riemann: "Kampf gegen die Alleinherrschaft des Klaviertones," *Musik*, IV (1905), 304 f.

[48] J. S. Bach ist often used as a basis for this view. The generally recognized authority on Bach, A. Schweitzer, on the other hand, has a different opinion and answers the question of what Bach might have thought of the modern piano in the following way: "Exactly the same as towards the modern organ. He would hail with enthusiasm the perfection of its mechanism, but not be particularly enchanted with its tone qualities." (Trans. E. Newman, I, New York, 1950, 352.)

W. Dirks adopts a similar point of view in a highly pertinent article, "Wo liegt die Grenze der Werktreue?," *Frankfurter Zeitung* (1940): "This statement can not be contradicted; the one person who could have done so died some hundred years before the development of the modern piano. Thus it is permissible to think up a reply for Bach—which, likewise, cannot be contradicted—such as the following: 'The fact that such compositions were written for the harpsichord and that the advantages as well as the drawbacks of the instrument have been taken into account by the composers.

With regard to the problem of harpsichord versus piano the clear characterizations of both instruments given by Eta Harich-Schneider may be cited: "Where does the beauty of the harpsichords's tone lie, in comparison to that of the well-known piano? What is the essential quality of the instrument? The modern piano is characterized by an orchestral fullness, its tone is soft and rounded, it has its velvety smoothness and singing quality, its gamut of dynamic effects and flexibility which permits a thousand gradations, a thousand variations in tone color. The modern piano seems to offer an invitation to penetrate the lyrical depths of one's own soul, to express one's self—it is, and despite its titanic power, it remains an intimate instrument. The piano has the capacity of flattering the ear—even when badly played it remains, in point of tone, quite bearable, becoming at the worst only bourgeois and conventional. The harpsichord, on the other hand, has its visor wide open. Its tone is not soft—it is sparkling, of a brittle purity. It is not round and not large, but it has a characteristic and inimitable spirituality which is touching because it cannot reveal its beauty through force, but only in the context of a clearly and distinctly articulated melodic line, like an unconscious attribute, hidden in the music. The colors of the various registers—the mildness of the eight foot, the rather bitter, incisive sweetness of the four foot, the dark quality of the sixteen foot, the humorous sharpness of a nasal register—all have their particular kind of reticence; they are of a proud race and wish to be known before they are loved and treasured. Indeed, the fact they are technically so difficult to manipulate is an indispensable aspect of these qualities. The very slight variations in dynamics possible on the harpsichord must to some extent be wooed before they respond. Yet it is they alone which impart that exceptional clarity to the long contrapuntal lines, which make the linear element

---

new pianos do not sound particularly good to me, in playing they are dull and unseemly loud. For the new ornamentations, which my sons prefer much more than I do myself, they are excellent. I will write Mr. Goldberg that he should play the Aria with Thirty Variations, which I composed for him, rather on the harpsichord. Perhaps soon I will compose something for the edification of those who like the new piano.'"

come to life, and through which the harpsichord can so purely entice the lover of early music."

It is from such points of view, established through historical studies, a keen sense of discrimination and a responsible attitude, that the modern building of harpsichords as well as other early keyboard instruments should proceed. To my way of thinking, fidelity to the actual sound of the original instrument is the first and highest task required of the modern builder of such instruments. I am by no means advocating a slavish copying of the early instruments, since such instruments produce total satisfaction neither for the builder nor for the player: not for the former, since even the most exact measurements of materials, such as wood, quills, leather, strings, etc., which have nothing in common with one another and which are nowadays manufactured in a totally different way, do not always produce satisfactory results; not for the latter, since in a real copy of this kind, the weak points would be reproduced as much as the strong ones, something that would in the long run attract only the most enthusiastic amateur builder. The reason that extant original instruments in museums or in private ownership are no longer satisfying is because certain characteristics that necessarily result from the manner of construction are now felt as shortcomings and weaknesses. Thus, early instruments in their original form suffer on account of being unable to stay in tune long enough, or being unable to maintain concert pitch, or from cracked sound boards, improper voicing in the jacks, uneven action of the keys, difficult or improper operation of the register stops and the considerable noise caused by the action. While some of these result from the age of the instruments, others are due to the fact that many technical methods used now were simply not at the avail of the original instrument builders and in consequence many aspects in the construction are quite rudimentary, even awkward and—this becomes clear when one examines the instruments themselves—are not at all well worked out. This must be stated in spite of all respect for the instrument builders of old.

Entirely different are the demands in our age of fine precision work. The use of modern techniques in the construction of harpsichords, however, should not lead us to make wholly new instruments which have nothing in common with their forerunners but the names. To this group belong instruments like the so-called substitute harpsichords,[49] which attempt to reproduce the characteristic tone by using specially constructed hammers or by the insertion of a jingling device between the hammers and the strings, attempts which even on the basis of purely acoustical considerations produce a tone quality quite different from the harpsichord, and thus were doomed from the very outset; and then all such instruments which incorporate qualities of the harpsichord in the modern piano (such as harpsichords whose dynamics may be varied,[50] or in an oversized iron frame, or with strings like those of a concert grand piano and others). Creations of this type, often requiring a not inconsiderable degree of inventiveness and ingenuity, were found satisfactory for a time, but they no longer suffice for present day conditions. In the struggle between the harpsichord and the piano for the rendition of early music, such an illegitimate instrument would not do much to advance the cause of the harpsichord. As with any musical instrument, the essential quality of the harpsichord lies in its sound, not in any external equipment added to satisfy the demands of a particular period.

A modern harpsichord, to be sucessful, must, on the one hand strictly preserve the old tone quality, that is, it must take over from the original the essential devices for the production of tone, such as the general shape, the arrangement of the strings, the registers, the plectrum action, but, on the other, it must be built in a technically precise and up-to-date fashion, making full use of modern methods. No deviations from the historical model should be allowed to cause any fundamental change in the quality of tone, but should rather provide greater ease in operation and a greater degree of reliability. Only an instrument of this kind, in essence true to tradition, but modern in technique, will be able to take its place along with the piano as the proper instrument for the performance of early music. [51]

---

[49] Among the first such attempts is the thumb tack piano, in which thumb tacks are pressed into the heads of the felt hammers in order to approach the dryness of tone characteristic of the harpsichord. Another is the *Cembalochord*, built by Glaser of Jena in 1928 under the guidance of Dr. Danckert and, finally, the modern electronic organs to the extent that they neglect their proper function and by special devices seek to imitate the sound of the harpsichord.

[50] For example, Mändler's *Bachklavier*, as described in *Die Musik* (1923), 792 f.

[51] The attitude of the writer on the problem of the reconstruction of early musical instruments has been summarized in the paper, "Kopie und Rekonstruktion," on the

Thus we have one guide to the solution of the various questions and problems in the building of harpsichords, a subject we will now take up in more detail. Still another basis is found in the early theoretical writings which discuss the problem, from which important passages have already been quoted in our technical description of the early keyboard instruments. And, finally, there are the early instruments themselves. [52] With regard to the latter, a certain amount of caution is indeed quite appropriate, more, to my way of thinking, than is usually exercised: one should not have an excessive respect for their great age. On the subject of making exact copies I have already mentioned a few matters and would like here to emphasize still a different point which is generally neglected: do these old instruments sound today the way they did originally? We, unfortunately, are not in the position that will be enjoyed by our posterity, who will be able to trace changes in the sounds of various instruments by means of phonograph records. Be this as it may, certain technical considerations point towards a negative answer for this question. Since a change in tone quality occurs over the years in any piano on account of the decreasing elasticity of the wood, it can certainly not be different in the case of the harpsichord, whose acoustical arrange-

---

occasion of the International Musicological Congress held in Bamberg in 1953 (see the *Kongressbericht*, Kassel–Basel, 1954) as well as in a reprint with added bibliography in *Instrumentenbauzeitschrift* (Konstanz, 1953, no. 1–2).

In the same *Kongressbericht* Alfred Berner in an article entitled "Die Instrumentenkunde in Wissenschaft und Praxis" states in regard to "the manufacturing of practical and playable instruments specially for the performance of early music, but for which contemporary composers also write" the following, which corresponds to the views of the present writer: "We must take as point of departure the fact that a mere copying of early instruments is not sufficient. As actual experience shows over and over again, we cannot be content with having merely translated the old literally into the present. This is possibly adequate in the case of scientific study; more generally it indicates an overemphasis upon history which is opposed not only to contemporary conditions but also to the normal development of the instrument itself, in which the process of technical improvement must not be overlooked. The following method should be chosen and indeed has already been employed: from the whole corpus of writing and analyses of music the most accurate possible conclusions are to be drawn, which make possible the construction of an instrument for the rendition of early music, but suited to contemporary conditions, by means of the careful employment of new technical methods and materials, and by taking into account certain modern requirements in regard to precision, tuning and cleaness in design."

[52] See Gurlitt, W.: "Der musikalische Denkmalswert der alten Musikinstrumente," *Neue Musikzeitung*, XLVIII (1927, no. 6).

ment is the same, but which is much older. Often the wood is dead and deviations from the original proportions can easily be seen in the bent and warped boards.

For this reason it is quite incorrect to demand that a newly built harpsichord should have the same quality of sounds as an old Ruckers instrument, since when it was new the Ruckers harpsichord sounded quite different from the way it does today. The proper demand addressed to the instrumental builder is to make a harpsichord that would correspond to the Ruckers instrument as it was in its prime. This task is far more difficult, since it requires one to uncover the essentiallly timeless aspects of the model and to choose properly what modifications must be introduced on the basis of a thorough knowledge of the instrument and of practical working experience. Thus it is quite understandable that in spite of many attempts, only a few builders have been successful[53] in the modern construction of early keyboard instruments. A good contemporary reconstruction is more than simply a pure mechanical copy.[54] Still further consideration should be given to the fact that our normal tuning of A (440 or 880 cycles per second) is substantially higher than that customary in the past. That such higher tuning had a negative influence on the sound quality of harpsichords can easily be seen from

---

[53] I will limit myself to a chronological listing of the following leading harpsichord builders: Pleyel (Paris, since 1888), Dolmetsch (Haslemere, since 1896; later with Chickering of Boston and Gaveau of Paris; in England again from 1914; he died in 1940), Johann George Steingraeber (Berlin; he died in 1932), Mändler (Munich; he died in 1958), and Neupert (Bamberg), the last three since about 1907.
On this subject, see an article by the present writer, "Cembalobau einst und jetzt," *Deutsche Tonkünstlerzeitung* (1937, no. 8). A more extensive discussion of modern harpsichords in comparison with the early instruments still extant is given by Wörsching: *Die historischen Saitenklaviere und der moderne Clavichord- und Cembalobau* (Mainz, 1946).
In addition to the above-mentioned older pioneers in modern harpsichord-building, in response to the lively interest and increased demand, a number of other firms have been formed over the years, many of which have already gone out of business; I will list these alphabetically: Ammer (Eisenberg), Challis (Detroit), Dowd (Boston), Feldberg (Sevenoaks), Glaser (Jena), Goble (Oxford), Goff (London), Gough (London), Hodsdon (Lavenham), Hubbard (Boston), Kemper (Lübeck), Merzdorf (Grötzingen), Sassmann (Remscheid), Schüler (Königsdorf), Sperrhake (Passau), Wittmayer (Gartenberg).
[54] Arnold Dolmetsch states on this subject: "I understood that copying other people's work, the best training for a beginner, should only be a step to higher achievements. The masters did not copy one another."

Praetorius' *Syntagma musicum* (1618), but this fact is rarely taken into account when old and modern instruments are compared. Anyone who tunes an old clavichord or harpsichord up as far towards modern concert pitch as the old strings and sound board permit, will be astonished at the change in tone quality produced by the added strain on the instrument and will no longer maintain that in modern instrument building it is sufficient to employ the older measurements, thicknesses of wood, etc., but rather that a well-thought-out proportional adaptation is unvoidable. Only a fanatical obsession with history lacking any knowledge of acoustics would deny this. Hence it is no crime against history (even though there are those who say the contrary) when minor changes are made in methods of arranging the strings, in the manner of construction and design of the casing, since these are undertaken solely because the original tone quality is to be achieved under contemporary conditions. The conscientious instrument builder must only be able to keep things in their proper perspective and not fall into the mistake of simply making a modern piano but with the harpsichord action. Another factor working in favor of a certain degree of freedom in building such instruments is that one cannot establish from the extant early instruments, nor from the various treatises, that there existed norms for the thicknesses of wood, measurements which were generally respected and rigidly maintained everywere; rather, there existed then, as now, individual technical differences not only between various builders but even between different instruments by one and the same builder, since uniform production in the modern sense was not known.

In the early treatises on instruments such differences are not concealed (one need only read the informative Adlung, who is frequently cited, in this connection)[55] but, within certain limits, a considerable degree of freedom in the arrangement of strings (the material used, its thickness, the way it is made), the thicknesses of wood and the general disposition

---

[55] Adlung's *Musica Mechanica Organoedi* (facsm. reprint, Kassel 1931) seems particularly noteworthy here, since there are some grounds for assuming that the views expressed in this work on *clavier* and organ building correspond to those of J. S. Bach. The manuscript which Adlung had prepared for publication at the time of his death (1762) was given to Bach's pupil, J. F. Agricola, with the request that any deviations from Bach's views on such matters should be added in the form of notes; the lack of such annotations can be taken as indicative of agreement. Adlung had himself been active as a builder of keyboard instruments.

was allowed, at all events more than is conceded today by many critics and musicologists who become involved in the competition between firms now engaged in the manufacture of harpsichords. Many such points of disagreement in regard to modern harpsichord building have taken on a significance that is quite irrelevant, since they have nothing to do with the most important issue, fidelity to the actual tone quality of the instrument. In regard to the matter of the proper disposition of the instrument, the great variety found in extant early harpsichords and the wishes of contemporary harpsichordists—both preclude an easy solution that will please everyone.

First of all the modern back (that is the entire bracing system or frame) comes to mind, as it is found on the larger contemporary harpsichords, particularly those intended for use in concert halls. There is no doubt that this back is much heavier than that found on early instruments. This, however, is its only drawback, since it has no influence on the tone quality, for it is not one of the vibrating and hence sounding parts of the instrument. Likewise the assumption that the closed sound chamber found on early instruments produces a totally different tone quality is not true at all in the larger instruments; on the contrary, the ability of modern instruments to carry is increased. Since the sound radiation is augmented by what comes from the open under side of the Soundboard. The most important technical advantage to be gained from the practice of employing a heavy back lies in the greater degree of stability that is attained for the more elaborate harpsichords. One must avoid the characteristic frequently found in early instruments and in modern ones that are built too lightly and without much thought, that the tension of the strings eventually causes the whole casing to warp out of shape. This not only alters the tone quality of the instrument, but interferes with the proper functioning of the various registers and with the ability of the instrument to remain in tune. A harpsichord that travels from concert to concert must be built more solidly than one which remains in the same place and is treated with proper care.

It is understandable that the attempt was made to increase the stability of the modern harpsichord by making use of an iron frame. Elsewhere[56]

---

[56] "Cembalo mit oder ohne Eisenrahmen," Zeitschrift für Instrumentenbau, L (1930, no. 2).

I have discussed this subject so that only the results need be given here. An iron frame—a frame in the real sense of the word and not merely iron plating or pieces of iron bracing here and there—never does any harm if it is properly built and in the case of special models using a great many strings it is even desirable. If it is not employed, other suitable technical methods, which likewise must be without influence on the tone quality, may be used, as in the support for the wrest plank and tuning pins, and for the 4' hitch pins,[57] to make these as secure as possible.[58] Such methods were even used on early harpsichords, so that they, as Adlung has it, "would last better." The question concerning the employment of iron has, on the whole, lost its importance since in general the concert type of instrument already described (with four sets of strings, five registers, six to eight pedals) has declined in significance. In defence of its honor, however, it must be stated that for forty years this type of concert harpsichord formed the vanguard in the struggle with the concert piano. Now that the harpsichord revival has been securely established, it is easy to push this instrument completely aside with a show of ingratitude coupled with superior knowledge, but I do not think it was dispensable at a time when the loudest instrument had the best chance for success, when there was no sign of any reduction in the sound and size of the orchestra and when almost all musical activity took place in the concert hall.

---

[57] Copyright feature of Neupert harpsichords.

[58] Another supporter of this strong type of construction is the scholar and harpsichordist Santiago Kastner (see his commentary to the *Tratado de la musica* of Bartolomeo Jobernardi, a member of the capella of Philip IV in Madrid in 1634: "Le clavecin parfait de B. Jobernardi," *Annuario musical*, VIII, Barcelona, 1953). He denies the validity of a *fidélité archéologique* in modern harpsichord building by referring to the construction of this *cimbalo perfetto*, which differs from its predecessors: three eight foot registers varying in tone quality, operated probably by knee-levers or pedals, at all events without interrupting the performance, a fairly silent action, more than usually reinforced by strong wooden braces (in the ribbing and back). Kastner thus presents modern harpsichord building with the challenge to employ again a *cadre de fonte réduit à son minimum indispensable*, thus a frame of light metal.

The observation that Spanish harpsichords had "more tone than any of the others" was made also by Burney on the occasion of his visit with Farinelli in Bologna in 1770. This corresponds to the findings of Ralph Kirkpatrick in his biography of Scarlatti (Princeton, 1953), that Domenico Scarlatti normally reckoned on a five octave harpsichord, using one manual but two eight foot registers.

It must not be forgotten that even in the past the disposition with two registers at eight foot, and one each at four and sixteen foot, as ascribed to Bach, Händel and Haydn, was relatively rare and thus all such instruments were regarded as large models and were precursors of the modern concert harpsichords. And when, in an advertisement announcing the sale of Händel's harpsichord in 1788 we read that it "has a powerful tone and is well calculated for concerts", then this instrument possessed, as far as I can see, the special acoustical, natural and technical characteristics of a modern concert harpsichord. All this, however, is stated only to defend the honour of a type of instrument that has by now gone out of favour.

Only two firms, to my knowledge, are now building harpsichords who employ iron plating and bracing; the demand for the use of but one material for the casing has long gone out of date. The danger of an injudicious use of iron seems to me to lie chiefly in the fact that it might lead to increasing the number of registers. This would mean greater tension *vis à vis* the instrument's frame and thus would require a far stronger sound board. The consequence is not only a coarsening of the tone quality, but also the loss of some of the upper partials (overtones), causing the tone colour to be more determined by the lower partials. This is the course that has been followed by the piano in the development to the modern concert instrument.

In our electronic age, however, there are more elegant solutions in situations where the use of one or more large harpsichords will not work, such as performances with a very large group of performers, or open-air concerts. For such events the present writer, working with Professor Trautwein on a performance of *Herakles* at the Dietrich-Eckhart Theater of the Olympiastadion in Berlin in 1936, developed in "Electric harpsichord."[59] This instrument, normal in its Ruckers disposition and its action, was protected from acoustical feedback and hollow resonances from above by thick padding and from below by a specially upholstered sound box. A microphone placed in this sound box picked up the sound, which was then electronically amplified and reproduced through eight loudspeakers placed above the orchestra and chorus.

---

[59] Concerning this, see Trautwein: "Dynamische Probleme der Musik," *Deutsche Musikkultur,* II (1937, no. 1).

Another method was employed by E. Thienhaus at concert given in the Schiller Theater of Berlin in 1940, in which two channel sound reproduction made its appearance, bringing with it a great improvement in the quality of sound through the stereophonic effects. [60]

I do not regard it as in any way improper, but rather as part of the revival of the harpsichord, if in the further development of the pure acoustic keyboard instruments (i. e., harpsichord, clavichord, piano) one seeks to build instruments weak in volume but noble in tone, then providing the necessary amplification by electronic means. This, however, assumes that the loudspeaker problem is solved so that the tone quality is accurately reproduced.

Otherwise we can state that the harpsichord, in contrast to the piano, "has proven itself to be the most naturally beautifully sounding instrument of all, and the one most suited to radio broadcasting," particularly through its tone character, the contrast of the registers, the elimination of the excessive use of the pedal, so characteristic of the piano, and, most especially, through the artistic value of the repertory of music for the instrument. [61]

We again encounter a difference of opinion in regard to the question of the use of register stops as opposed to pedals. For the technician there is no problem, since neither presents any difficulty today and both can even be combined when so desired. The objection to the pedal arises rather from artistic and stylistic considerations. It is said that the assignment of changing register to the foot makes such a shift so easily and, from the historical viewpoint, improperly available, that in effect a superabundance of registrations would exist, so that the newly gained stylistic feeling would be lost and the reputation of the instrument would suffer. The danger of misuse is from the technical point of view no proper reason for a general condemnation. It seems to me, futhermore, that such a conservative point of view, which would not permit the use of any technical advances on a harpsichord, has the effect of jeopardizing its position in its rivalry with the piano far more than would a harpsi-

---

[60] See the report by Thienhaus: "Konzertmäßige Zweikanalschallübertragung für das Cembalo," *Akustische Zeitschrift*, VI (1941, no. 1).
[61] See Szendrei: *Rundfunk und Musikpflege* (Leipzig, 1931).

chord whose registration is somewhat elaborate, since modern man has become accustomed to technical methods for making things easier. One should regard an excessive use of register changes in a performance of Bach on a harpsichord as preferable to a more romantic one on a piano. The distance from an excessive use of register pedals on a harpsichord to a well thought-out, sparing and stylistically pure manner of playing (making use, however, of terrace dynamics, although with less differentiation between the various degrees) is less than that from the piano to an awkward harpsichord with the old stops on the sides or within the instrument case. For these reasons I maintain that for the largest harpsichords pedals are advisable (at least for the various sounding registers; for coloristic registers, like buff and piano stops, manual levers work well enough) and for smaller models, manual stops operated from the front are sufficient.[62] Coupling two manuals in the former is best accomplished by pedals or knee-levers, in the latter by sliding the manuals. Let it be repeated that technically any combinations are possible.

The use of pedals for register changes was not wholly unknown in the past: as has previously been stated, in Mace's *Musick's Monument* John Hayward, a Londoner, is mentioned as having been the inventor and builder of such a harpsichord around 1660 ("A most excellent kind of instrument for a concert") with four "pummels of wood" for the production of "varieties with the foot"; we also know that the Parisian harpsichord builder Taskin (1723—1795) in conjunction with the gradual expansion of the compass of the instrument employed "méchaniques au pied pour varier le jeu de 10 à 12 manières"; instruments built by Shudi and Broadwood with pedals for lute and swell registers have been preserved, as has a two manual harpsichord with pedal registration built by Sebastian Erard in 1779. The lack of pedals on earlier instruments may perhaps be easily explainable technically by stating that a suitable manner for making a lyre secure had not been worked out and that at the very beginning there existed no great stylistic demand for such pedals. That the use of pedals was found not disadvantageous is proven

---

[62] A valuable improvement in a one manual harpsichord without pedals, can be brought about by the use of an eight foot register with a piano stop controlled by a knee-lever (as, for example, the former Neupert-Bärenreiter harpsichord), which would accomplish without interrupting the playing effects that otherwise would require a two manual instrument.

68

by a statement in Adlung's *Anleitung zur musikalischen Gelahrtheit*: "...something much more pleasing to me (is) when such changes of register can be made unnoticed while playing, without the use of the hands."

Philipp Emanuel Bach is likewise in favor of this: "The fine invention of our celebrated Holefeld which makes it possible to increase or decrease the registration by means of pedals, while playing, has made the harpsichord, particularly the single-manual kind, a much-improved instrument, and, fortunately, eliminated all difficulties connected with the performance of a piano. If only all harpsichords were similarly constructed as a tribute to good taste." [62a] Similarly [63] in a newspaper report probably written by Leopold Mozart concerning the playing of the prodigy Wolfgang an a Shudi harpsichord built for Frederick the Great states: "One notices as something rather extraordinary that Herr Tschudi has all registers operated by pedal, so that they can be made to sound one after the other simply by pressing with the foot and an increase or decrease in volume can be produced at will, a crescendo and decrescendo long desired by harpsichordists." Knee-levers on harpsichords are known to have existed, such as the "registre mû par le genou" by Berger of Grenoble in 1765 and the "bascules actionées par les genoux" by Virbès in 1766, but they in all probability are of even earlier origin, since they are simpler than pedals.

In regard to further technical improvements in the modern harpsichord, I would like briefly to mention the following: it is now customary to make the jack slides of metal, which allows greater accuracy in the motion of the jacks and also lessens the possibility of sticking due to humidity; alternatively, the jack itself can be made of metal or of non-hygroscopic materials (such as synthetic resin or moulded plastic). One also can find an arrangement employing springs, adjusted by a device to allow the quill to fall past the string without touching it on the return to its original position. All points of possible friction and contact are carefully fitted to reduce the not inconsiderable sound of the plectrum action to the absolute minimum. On account of its greater durability, leather is almost exclusively used for the plectra; we have become so skilled in the

---

[62a] Bach, *op. cit.*, 368–369.
[63] See Kinsky: "Mozartinstrumente," *Acta Musicologica*, XII (1940), 1 f.

manufacture of this leather that the sound it produces differs in no way from that of a real quill plectrum. The adjustment of the force with which the strings are plucked, the distance they rise and the degree of damping are adjusted, for individual jacks as well as for entire registers, by minute regulating screws and other precise adjustment devices. The constant aim (at least, of the best manufacturers; there are, unfortunately, also firms that turn out an inferior, short-lived product, a counterfeit to history!) is that the playing and care of the instrument is made as easy as possible, since all instruments of the harpsichord family require careful and understanding treatment. As an early writer states, "It is a sweet but highly fickle instrument," an "instrument that is always changing, now here and now there . . ."[64] and this is to some extent true of modern harpsichords, since many such weaknesses must be regarded as quite unavoidable.[65] One must not attribute the characteristics of a piano, which has to be built more strongly and roughly, to a modern harpsichord. The extremely delicate action, which is compounded of minute parts, the thin sound board, the weakness of the strings, which in many registers are thinner than the weakest string of the piano, the use of nothing but wood in the construction of the case—all these produce a certain sensibility.

In this connection let us make a few remarks about tuning the harpsichord and its ability to maintain pitch. As early as 1387 John I of Aragon recommended that a newly acquired *exaquier* be treated with care; the theorist Zarlino in 1558 demanded of a good musician the ability to tune a harpsichord himself; in 1618 Praetorius speaks of the "great difficulty and misery" caused by harpsichords and spinets "with quills, often requiring correction and retuning"; Mersenne in his *Harmonie universelle* (1636) states that a harpsichord which is properly built, well tuned and carefully looked after should stay in tune for a period of one to two weeks; in the early 17th century there were professional harpsichord

---

[64] Fuhrmann: *Musikalischer Trichter* (Frankfurt a. O., 1706).

[65] The general validity of this statement is supported in Ehlers: *Cembalo* (Wolfenbüttel, 1933): "Thus there is and always should be in all good harpsichords a remnant of the perception of these technical characteristics, only to be overcome by devoted and understanding treatment on the part of the player. The harpsichordist must have a strong material relation to his instrument along with the purely artistic; he must be a bit of a putterer."

tuners in the St. Luke guild "Claversigelstelder" in Amsterdam; J.S. Bach took it upon himself to tune and look after the plectra on his own instruments, since no one else could satisfy him;[66] even the most fully developed and stable among early harpsichords, those made in England in the latter half of the 18th century, require similar care. We learn from Tschudi's biographer Dale, that according to the account book, for a quarter of a year at least six tunings were carried out, but that many harpsichord owners had their instruments tuned and adjusted every week at a cost of 2s. 6d. per time. Dr. Burney, whom we have already mentioned, emphasizes the fact that the four foot register is "much affected by the least change in the temperature of air, that it is almost instantly discovered when there was a change in the wind." Hipkins, one of the finest historians of keyboard instruments, is not wholly wrong in his article on Shudi in *Grove's Dictionary* when he states that at the time harpsichords were really intended for wealthy people, on the one hand because of their high cost relative to the value of currency at the time and on the other hand because of the many expenses and other things that arose from their proper maintenance: the cost of tuning and repairing a harpsichord for a year could easily have fed a man. Adlung is quite detailed on this point: "Tuning must take place shortly before the instrument is needed and one must not carry it to the place where it is to be used until just before the performance is to commence. Otherwise the changes in the air, or where it is more humid, will quickly cause it to go out of tune. If, as is probable, this place is more humid than where the instrument was tuned, one should leave the harpsichord with its lid down, particularly when

---

[66] Forkel states in his Bach biography (Kassel, 1925; English translation in David-Mendel: *The Bach Reader*, New York, 1945): "Nobody could install the quill-plectrums to his satisfaction; he always did it himself. He also tuned both his harpsichord and his clavichord himself, and was so practiced in the operation that it never cost him above a quarter of an hour."
In this connection Albert Schweitzer states: "In that epoch every artist was still to some extent an instrument maker, and every instrument maker to some extent an artist. It was at least expected of every capable player that he should be able to keep his instrument in repair..." (Trans. E. Newman, I, New York, 1950, 59.)
A certain amount of knowledge concerning the technical operation of the harpsichord is just as important for the modern player as it is for the manufacturer to know something of artistic matters. A mutual exchange of ideas would only be of the greatest value in the harpsichord field at large, but practical aspects of actual production should always be left to the specialist.

it is to be played on a lawn. Otherwise it must be transported there well in advance and, after having been allowed to go fully out of tune, must once again be properly tuned. The night is cooler than the day, a fact which will easily produce a change. For the sound board of the harpsichord is highly individual and it contracts; under the moist air the strings relax. If a *clavier* (clavichord) or *clavecin* (harpsichord) is to sound properly, it must always be kept clean and often be tuned."[67]

Humidity and change in temperature may quite properly be described as having the worst effect upon the ability of the harpsichord and related instruments to remain in tune, as well as their ability to give service over a period of many years. Any layman will see that a string with a diameter of .2 millimeter in four foot pitch, strung over wood, on a weak base and pressed tight against a bridge, with a tension of about nine pounds (4.5 kilograms) and constantly plucked, will react more than will the strong steel string of a piano, built on an iron frame, led over a strong arched support with firm bracing, which is struck by felt hammers. Anyone who refuses to accept this is in effect demanding the repeal of natural physical laws.

Finally, the question of disposition is a significant one for the modern building of harpsichords. This problem is most easily and satisfactorily solved today by incorporating into the instrument all those features which seem to have been the most characteristic on the basis of early instruments that are still extant (see the table on p. 33/34). Here it is not a question of making exact copies, since new demands in connection with modern use of the instrument can easily be met even though these characteristic features are maintained. It seems to be a consequence of such demands that today the need for two manual harpsichords with two registers at eight foot, one at four and one at sixteen is much greater than would be excepted on the basis of conditions prevailing in the 18th century. On the one hand the modern harpsichordist has at his avail a repertory of music from three centuries that is constantly growing, but on the other, he is almost never in the fortunate position of many of the

---

[67] In 1724 an organist in Braunschweig, H. L. Hurlebusch, wrote to his Town Council that he required an extra amount, to the amount of a *taler*, for his harpsichord playing, since he "worked many hours on the maintenance of the instrument and also ran some danger in carrying it here and there if this large and expensive mechanism were ever to be damaged."

older musicians who owned several instruments of the harpsichord family for various purposes.

Therefore, one requires an instrument which combines the qualities of different models, one that can be used for simple virginal music as well as for the subtle rendition of French *clavecin* music and, finally, for the stylistically proper performance of the works of Bach, not a penetrating and piercing sound, but one that is bright, singing and clear, and which at the same time possesses sufficient fullness and carrying power for concert use.

The disposition best suited for so many different purposes has proven, now as well as in the past, to be the old Ruckers disposition with two manuals, two registers at eight foot and one at four. The writer believes he has come close to this ideal type in the "Couperin" model made by the Neupert Company, since this model combines a rich number of registration possibilities with the smaller size generally desired today (thirty-six by seventy-five inches) and a moderate price. The eight foot register of the lower manual is open and solid, while the other, operated from the upper manual, is more nasal, like the oboe; the loudness of both may be altered in stages by a piano mechanism operated manually by means of stops; a harp stop on the first eight foot register offers still additional variety. The four foot choir, normally operated from the lower manual, may also be played from the upper, which is arranged so that it will slide. Apart from this there is a manual coupler, also operated by a hand stop, making all three registers playable from the lower manual. The following possibilities exist:

Without coupling:	8^1, 8^1p, 8^1L, 8^1pL, 4, 8^2, 8^2p, 8^1+4, 8^1p$+4$, 8^1L$+4$, 8^1pL$+4$
With slide coupling:	8^2+4, 8^2p$+4$
With manual coupling:	8^1+8^2, 8^1p$+8^2$, 8^1L$+8^2$, 8^1pL$+8^2$, 8^1+8^2p, 8^1p$+8^2$p, 8^1L$+8^2$p, 8^1pL$+8^2$p, 8^1+8^2+4, 8^1p$+8^2+4$, 8^1L$+8^2+4$, 8^1pL$+8^2+4$, 8^1+8^2p$+4$, 8^1p$+8^2$p$+4$, 8^1L$+8^2$p$+4$, 8^1pL$+8^2$p$+4$

p = piano stop
L = harp stop

Thus, in all, twenty-nine combinations.

The combination of a beautiful silvery tone with the richness of colour of the larger models is what caused J. Adlung to praise this arrangement particularly in his *Musica Mechanica Organoedi* (1768), no. 511. And elsewhere, in no. 246 of his *Musikalische Gelahrtheit*, he goes so far as to call a harpsichord arranged in this way the "most beautiful harpsichord" ("schönste clavessin") that he ever saw or heard. The fact that Adlung's views on organ and *clavier* building probably correspond to those of J. S. Bach has already been mentioned (see footnote 55).

For one manual harpsichords, most usual is a disposition with an eight and a four foot register, to which additional variety is given by buff stops, often divided between treble and bass; a substitute for the echo effect normally provided by the second manual can be produced by a piano stop operated manually or by the knee.

Among the smaller models, spinets and spinettinos enjoy a growing reputation as simple domestic instruments for solo playing and accompaniments, perhaps on account of their reasonable price. The astonishing carrying power of their tone, the ease with which they can be transported in a suitcase or trunk, and their great stability in spite of it all, often allow these small models to fill in successfully in the absence of larger instruments. Furthermore, combinations of two such instruments, whether two at eight foot pitch or one at eight and the other at four have been built with one placed upon the other. Recently the writer has arranged an eight foot spinet so that it may not only be used by itself, but also so that it may be attached to another instrument and thus can be used as a third manual to an otherwise two manual harpsichord.

In the early days of the harpsichord revival concert instruments used a disposition employed by Pleyel, consisting of five registers, one each at four, eight and sixteen foot, on the lower manual and two eight foot registers on the upper manual, one piano, the other nasal. This arrangement has now been rejected for tonal and stylistic reason on account of the conglomeration of registers on the lower manual.[68] Today the ideal concert instrument is a two manual harpsichord with a keyboard range of five octaves in the Bach disposition (already described), which is often

---

[68] On this, see Matthaei: "Über Cembaloneukonstruktionen," *Zeitschrift für Hausmusik*, II (1933, no. 5–6).

modified by the use of theorboe or buff stops on the sixteen foot register and by other means. With two piano and two buff stops, eighty-eight various registration possibilities exist.

The use of the sixteen foot register raises several questions, such as whether the old masters ever prescribed or recognized the use of this register. One should always remember that in the past composers always figured upon the use of instruments with widely differing dispositions. There certainly are a number of places in the organ literature where the sixteen foot stop is called for, as has already been discussed by Harich-Schneider (op. cit., chapter 7). On the basis of the fact that in previous centuries the various keyboard instruments were not differentiated as they are today, it can be maintained that what was said of the organ sixteen foot register would also apply to that on a harpsichord: it should be used whenever it was found on an instrument, but not as a generally binding rule. There is no assurance in this regard even in the case of J. S. Bach, since the Berlin instrument has not been authenticated[69] and the Silbermann harpsichord is in the Eisenach Bach house by pure chance. From the inventory of the possessions left by him we can establish only that there were six harpsichords, four large, one smaller and one spinet. However, it is highly probable that J. S. Bach knew and played instruments with the sixteen foot register even if he did not himself own one, since he took an active interest in innovations and other aspects of instrument building (I am thinking here of his approval of the earliest pianos, of his commissioning of Silbermann's pupil Zacharias Hildebrandt to build a lute harpsichord) and since he knew Gottfried Silbermann who built harpsichords with a sixteen foot register. Furthermore, as an organist, he had a definite interest in the enrichment of the harpsichord registers.

The situation is similar with Händel, who was a friend of Burcat Shudi, the most famous instrument builder in England at the time and particularly known for his large instruments. Handel played not only Ruckers instruments but also those made by Shudi. In Händel's case, however, it is not mere guesswork as it was in that of Bach, since proof is given

---

[69] See Kinsky: "Zur Echtheitsfrage des Berliner Bachflügels," *Bach-Jahrbuch* (1924) and Kreichgauer: "Ist der Berliner Bachflügel echt?," *Deutsche Tonkünstler-Zeitung* (1938, no. 8). For further interesting investigations concerning the manuals, range and disposition of Baroque instruments in particular, see F. Ernst: *Der Flügel J. S. Bachs* (Frankfurt, 1955).

through an advertisement in an English newspaper. Philip James, in his *Early Keyboard Instruments* (London, 1930), p. 42, refers to an announcement for an auction in the *Morning Herald* (London, June 26, 1788) containing the following: "A Capital double Key'd Harpsichord by Burcat *(sic)* Schudi, made for the Immortal Händel and used by him till his death, at the different Concerts in London. It consists of four stops, which are as follow: two unisons, an upper and lower octave, has a powerful tone and is well calculated for Concerts." Hence, without doubt: two manuals with four registers: two at eight foot, and one each at four and sixteen foot.

A similar newspaper announcement regarding a harpsichord with a sixteen foot stop is found in the *Public Ledger* (London, October 2, 1778): "A remarkable fine toned Harpsichord by Ephraim Celson, an instrument of a most extraordinary construction and justly esteemed the most compleat harpsichord of the kingdom: it contains a double bass, two unisons and a octave . . ." Thus "extraordinary" to be sure, but yet, a register at sixteen foot, two at eight foot, and one at four foot.

The same impression, that instruments with the sixteen foot register were generally known without being common, can be seen elsewhere, in places I will simply mention here: the *Encyclopédie* of Diderot and D'Alembert (Paris, 1751—1777) mentions particularly a "bourdon de 16 pieds" in the article "Clavecin."

In his *De l'Harmonie universelle* (Paris, 1637) Mersenne writes: "It seems to me that musicians of the preceding century had neither harpsichords nor *épinettes* with two or more manuals, as we have today, with four manuals and four sets of strings, of whom the largest correspond to the twelve of the organ." Adlung's *Anleitung zur musikalischen Gelahrtheit* (1758) contains the passage already cited (see footnote 27). In his *Musica Mechanica Organoedi* (1768) Adlung also gives a description of a harpsichord made by Breitenbach with registers at four, eight and sixteen foot pitch. This passage is also mentioned by Oscar Paul in his *Geschichte des Klaviers* (Leipzig, 1868): "At times they even used a coupling similar to that on organs, and could have all three registers, at four, eight and sixteen foot, sound at one and the same time, as was observed by Adlung on a Breitenbach harpsichord."

W. A. Mozart in a letter to his father in 1781 writes that he had two harpsichords in his quarters on the *Petersplatz* at Vienna, "one for 'galanterie' playing, and the other a *Maschine* provided throughout with a lower octave, tuned like the one we had in London, hence like an organ; on this I have also improvised and played fugues." Thus, in all probability a two manual harpsichord with a sixteen foot register and pedals or knee-levers *(Maschine)*.

Hipkins, in his *A Description and History of the Pianoforte* (London, 1896) states: "Some large German harpsichords had not only the two unison registers and an octave one equivalent to eight and four foot stops, but also a Bourdon, answering to sixteen foot pitch."

Arnold Dolmetsch, in his *The Interpretation of Music of the 17th and 18th Centuries* (London, 1915), has: "Some harpsichords possessed an additional fourth row of strings, placed above the unisons and double their length or thereabouts, giving 16 ft. tone. These instruments were necessarily very large and never became common, but they had a wonderful depth and grandeur of tone."

With this passage we have at least reached a judgment concerning the sixteen foot register: it has significance as a register that provides a solid acoustical foundation and augments the dynamic range, especially useful as a reserve of sound potentiality in concert instruments; it also provides an enrichment of the available range of tone color, particularly through combinations with a four foot register, through a lute effect (theorboe stop) or by transposing solo playing up an octave (bassoon-like sound). It should also be mentioned, however, that its presence means an expansion in compass by an octave in the bass, so that, for example, a harpsichord with a keyboard range of five octaves but with registers at four, eight and sixteen foot pitch actually possesses a range of seven octaves.

The stylistic problem of the sixteen foot register is accompanied by a technical one, namely, how to produce a good homogenous sound from all four registers of a harpsichord which has such a sixteen foot register. Several contradictory factors have to be resolved in the building of this kind of instrument: if it is to sound well and to accomplish the role of providing an accoustical support and tonal filling, the sixteen foot register must have a certain minimum length. If this is not met, the thickly wound strings will produce more extraneous noise than actual musical tone. On the other hand, it is not desirable for a concert harpsichord to be more than eight feet long. Furthermore, a certain maximum length is fixed by the breaking point of the very fine strings used in the treble of the eight and four foot registers. In addition, the jack slides themselves must be of a certain width, the sound board bridges must be located at acoustically favorable points and not be too close to one another and, finally, the placing of the jacks in relation to the lengths of the strings must be done in accordance with the desired tone quality. If the vibrations of the strings and the sound board require strings of unusual strength, this added strain will affect the whole four foot register as well as the entire five octave compass and hence will necessitate another adjustment, either the use of stronger wood or a special procedure in regard to the hitch pins. At present the general belief is that for concerts in large halls a harpsichord must have this keyboard compass of five octaves and the corresponding total range of seven octaves. Indeed, referring to certain passages in Domenico Scarlatti it seems advisable to extend the range of the eight foot register to g'''. Happily it is now being realized that for normal purposes a range of four and a half octaves (C to f''') is quite sufficient. The limit of four octaves on earlier instruments is no longer good enough and was rejected even by Adlung.

After the description of all these technical difficulties, it is doubtless readily understandable that an arrangement with one register at eight, four and sixteen foot pitch respectively is better acoustically as well as technically. It has been used in modern harpsichord construction, but— as was true in the past (see the table giving the various dispositions)— has never attained any particular importance. The writer sees the explanation for this to lie in the fact that today the absence of the second eight foot register is keenly felt, since the present ideal tends toward a contrast in tone colour, which can be well achieved by two eight foot registers differentiated in character from one another. Accordingly he has produced a variation from the Bach disposition in the Neupert Harpsichord Model B/K (Bach Concert) by altering the tone colour of the eight foot stop in the upper manual, which formerly differed from that of the lower only in its dynamic level, towards a nasal quality, rich in overtones.

In this case the upper manual is not regarded as secondary and softly voiced to serve as an echo, but should be considered dynamically equal to the other; dynamic alterations are taken care of by piano stops. This follows the prototype of the Baroque organ, in which a rather dull but solid principle section is complemented by a bright secondary section rich in overtones.

Finally we must mention the various dispositions in pedal harpsichords which will serve to round out the harpsichord family as it is being built today. These have registers at eight and sixteen foot pitch, or at four, eight and sixteen foot pitch and with the Venetian Swell. Such a pedal in conjunction with a modern concert harpsichord produces hundreds of possible tone combinations and thus a richness of colour and splendour of tone which makes the instrument approach the organ, to which its so closely related in the matter of general music style.

In summary it can be said that great attention has always been paid to the question of disposition, in the past as well as among the responsible instrument builders of the present day.[70] The value of a good disposition is seen to lie in bringing the selection and arrangement of registers, manuals and other devices, into harmony with the tonal, stylistic and technical requirements by the proper use of all available modern technical methods.

To give a picture of how the whole modern harpsichord familiy is arranged, I will indicate the scheme followed by the Neupert Company in Bamberg:

Spinettino

$1 \times 4'$ Harp stop

Spinet   4 octaves

$1 \times 8'$ Divided harp stop

$4^{1}/_{2}$ to 5 octaves

---

[70] See Neupert: "Ueber Cembalodispositionen," *Deutsche Instrumentenbauzeitung* (1937, no. 5—6). Also: Ernst: *Vom Cembalo* (Zürich, 1946). A further contribution to the question of contemporary harpsichord building is available among the reports of the English Musical Association, C. V. Pilkington: *The Harpsichord: Its Present and its Future* (London, 1935).

Harpsichord (one manual)

$1 \times 8'$, $1 \times 4'$,   Divided harp stop, 8' piano stop

Harpsichord (two manuals) Ruckers disposition

Upper manual: $1 \times 8'$, piano stop
Lower manual: $1 \times 8'$, piano stop, harp stop
$1 \times 4'$ (transmission to upper manual)
Manual coupling

Harpsichord (two manuals) Bach disposition

Upper manual: $1 \times 8'$, $1 \times 4'$; 8' piano stop; harp stop
Lower manual: $1 \times 8'$, $1 \times 16'$; 8' piano stop; theorboe stop
Manual coupling

Keyboard range:
$4^1/_2$ to 5 octaves
Total range: up to
7 octaves F_2 to f'''')

Pedal harpsichord, 27 or 30 tones (c—d or f)

$1 \times 8'$, $1 \times 4'$, $1 \times 16'$, Venetian Swell

A relative newcomer is the *cembalino*, a small upright harpsichord developed by the Neupert Company in 1957—1958 (both the name and the modification of the plectrum action are copyright).[70a] This instrument is particularly well suited to those who want a small one manual harpsichord with a disposition of one eight and one four foot choir of strings and a keyboard compass of four and a half to five octaves, but who have only a limited space available for such an instrument.

While in many respects it is the same as any harpsichord (wooden casing, wrest plank, strings, sound board, tuning pins, bridges, etc.), its plectrum action is entirely different, preserving only that one indispensable feature—the plucking of the strings. Here there are no jack guides or jack rails, not even any jacks: of the usual plectrum action there remain only the tongues with their attached plectra which pluck the strings in the course of their front-to-back motion.

[70a] A description of the early history and development of the *cembalino* is given by the writer: "Das Clavicytherium einst und heute," *Musica* (1958, no. 6), 333 f.

As with all contemporary versions of early musical instruments, the modern harpsichord is chiefly designed to present works of early music in their purest form. A constantly growing number of enthusiastic artists and their followers are working in this way and thus are bringing forgotten musical compositions to new life. If it should go beyond this purpose by creating a new and characteristic art in modern music from the influence of the old strict form, then its revitalization would not be fruitless, either for the past or the future. I believe that in this regard the harpsichord has a certain importance at the present time, since in its very essence it inclines to honorable craftsmanship and to an intimate and close feeling of community. Such a strength, more communal than social, may also contribute to overcome the separation between everyday life and art, under which we suffer greatly today, and to bring both together again in the close relationship they once enjoyed.

THE CARE OF MODERN HARPSICHORDS AND OTHER INSTRUMENTS WITH PLECTRUM ACTION

The harpsichord and the smaller spinet, spinettino and virginal, require at least the same careful treatment that would be accorded any keyboard instrument. Certain technical features (the wooden construction, delicate sound board and sets of strings, plectrum action) require in addition special care, the particulars of which should be known not only to the technician and repair man but to the harpsichordist himself, at least in their most basic aspects. This holds not only for the older instruments that have been preserved but also for contemporary models, even though modern technical methods have where possible ameliorated or at least substantially simplified and refined the manner of construction and operation.

To treat a harpsichord properly one must have a sound knowledge of its principal parts and how the operate. Even Adlung, although in reference to organ building but with application to harpsichords, states: "Beyond a recognition of the various registers I require also additional knowledge, so that a lover of keyboard instruments will not damage his instrument through carelessness, but will be able to maintain it and even to make minor repairs when necessary."

Description of the Construction of a Harpsichord

The supporting structure of the harpsichord is a wooden frame, covered by an outer casing on the top and sides and sometimes closed in on the bottom. It supports the wrest-plank and the soundboard and, therefore, the tension of the strings, since the strings extend from rotatable pins, called tuning pins, set into the wrest-plank, over the wrest-plank bridge, and across the soundboard to the soundboard bridge, where single or staggered bridge-pins determine the exact length of the vibrating portions, and finally end by being looped around hitch-pins, which are arranged anlong the inner laminated rim of the casing. This applies to the eight and sixteen foot registers (eight foot is normal pitch, sixteen foot sounds an octave lower); but the shorter four foot strings, sounding an octave higher than the eight foot, have their own bridge and are either hitched to the soundboard itself or to hitch-pins extending through holes in the soundboard from a special frame built underneath. The strings are made of steel or brass, and in the lower registers they are overwound with fine-gauge wire of brass, copper, or silver-plated copper.

Underneath at the front the frame is held together by the keybed, upon which is built the keyboard, a system of levers which transmit motion to the plectrum action. The keyboard consists of one or two manuals having a compass which varies according to the size and purpose of the instrument (normally on the larger instruments $4^1/_2$ to 5 octaves, or 54 to 61 keys per manual, and 4 octaves, or 49 keys, on spinettinos and virginals). In two-manual instruments there is usually a manual coupler. On the padded, far ends of the keys rest the jacks, which contain the plectrum action. The jacks themselves are narrow pieces of wood, metal, or plastic and have a tongue mounted on a pivot in a mortise near the upper end. The plectrum projects at right angles from this tongue and is made of either feather-quill, plastic, or specially selected and prepared leather. On the side opposite the plectrum, the tongue contains a notch against which a spring made of metal or hogbristle bears, pressing the tongue's lower, leather-padded, oblique end against a corresponding oblique cut in the jack. A small set-screw threaded through the body of the jack to the oblique cut in the mortise regulates the distance the plectrum protrudes from the axis of the jack (see fig. 5)

The actual operation of the plectrum action is as follows: When the key is depressed, the plectrum, which is immediately below the string, rises and plucks the string in passing, setting it into motion. The distance which the jack rises is limited by the dip, or distance the key can be depressed, and by the position of the jack-rail above the jack. When the key is released the jack drops back again, and the plectrum, owing to the pivoting of the tongue, passes the string without plucking it. A felt damper at the top of the jack damps the strings's vibrations; the spring against the tongue makes the jack ready for use again. The return of the jack and the consequent damping are often facilitated by a lead weight inserted in the lower portion of the jack.

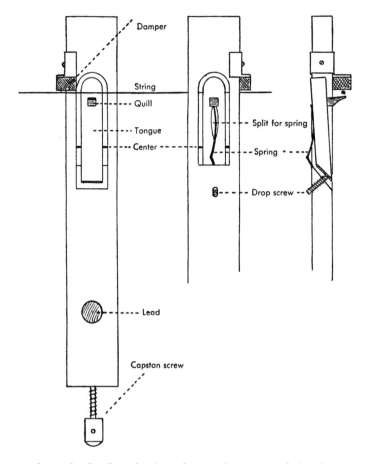

Damper

String

Quill

Tongue

Center

Lead

Capstan screw

Split for spring

Spring

Drop screw

Fig. 5. A harpsichord jack made of wood or synthetic material (for the most recent metal jack, see the picture at he end of the book).

The position of the plectrum relative to the string and the moment of attack are regulated by a capstan screw threaded into the bottom of the jack. Capstan screws are head-screws with lateral holes. The distance the plectrum protrudes, and hence the strength with which it plucks, is controlled by the set- or dropscrew against the tongue, as has already been mentioned. The vertical motion of the jack is guided by openings in

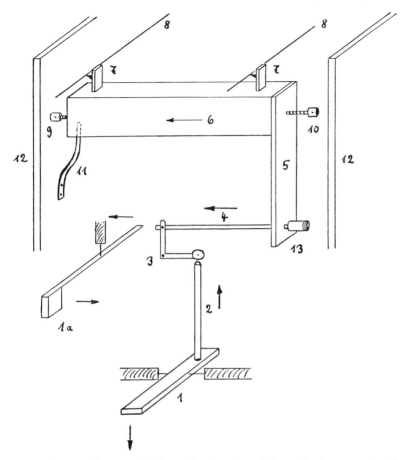

Fig. 6. Schematic diagram of a harpsichord register slide mechanism, operating by means of (1) pedal and (1a) knee-lever

1. Pedal, 1 a. Knee lever, 2. Bar or rod, 3. Right angle lever, 4. Transmission, 5. Slide pole, 6. Jack slide 7. Jacks, 8. Strings, 9. Capstan screw (in), 10. Capstan screw (out), 11. Spring on jack slide, 12, Casing, 13. Regulating screw.

the jack-slides, or jack-guides. Every sounding register is provided with such a jack-slide. In instruments having but one register, such as spinets, spinettinos, and virginals, this slide is fixed in position, but on instruments with several registers, the slides move laterally at right angles to the strings. The slides are positioned between the wrest-plank and the front cross-beam of the frame, upon which the front end of the soundboard is fastened. It is possible to slide whole registers so far to one side that their plectra do not reach the strings and in consequence do not sound, and the reverse, of course, can also be accomplished. Adjusting screws regulate the amount of travel in both directions, and a return to the proper position is frequently accomplished by a spring when the lever or pedal controlling the slide is released. The operation of the jack-slide is controlled by hand-stops located on the nameboard above the keys, by kneelevers under the key-bed, or by pedals at the base of the instrument.

Various combinations as well as varied types of transmission systems, such as rods, levers, handscrews, oblique slides, etc., are therefore possible. Similar arrangements operate mechanical registers like the lute stop, which, by causing a strip of felt to touch the strings near the bridge, alters the sound of the eight foot register to resemble that of the lute and of the sixteen foot register to that of the theorboe; the piano stops cause a partial shifting of a register to reduce the volume; manual coupling, by means of a transmission mechanism, causes the keys of the upper manual to be operated by the lower manual. Coupling is sometimes accomplished by employing the simpler medium of sliding in the whole upper keyboard.

Except for its external appearance, we have discussed the important details of the construction of a harpsichord. Anyone who has gained some understanding of how the instrument works, by means of the schematic diagrams followed up where possible by actual examination of a harpsichord, will be in a position to understand the following remarks on the proper treatment of such instruments. In any case, he will not be helpless with a harpsichord and can always have a good and playable instrument at his disposal. A sensitive regard for its technical needs will be reflected by the instrument itself, just as ignorant treatment will be answered in kind.

The Care and Treatment of Harpsichords

1. Careful attention must begin when the instrument itself arrives. It should actually be superfluous to mention that the instrument when packed in its case must not be dropped or thrown around during transportation. Even so, it is recommended that the carrier's attention be called to this fact, although it is probably indicated by stickers on the packing case. At all events, any external damage to the instrument or to its packing (broken boards, signs of dampness) should be pointed out in the presence of the delivery man and then officially so that any insurance claims made by the recipient will be honored. Faint little marks on the exterior of the packing case, minor scratches and other things which any carpenter can easily take care of are naturally not to be included under such transportation damages.

2. For unpacking, the case is to be lain right side up, the top taken off and upon the removal of the packing material the instrument itself can be lifted out. The legs are screwed on and secured as indicated by the designations which correspond to those on the under side of the instrument. With instruments having pedals, the lyre is to be screwed on firmly and fastened with the bracing provided. If kneelevers are involved, the protecting blocks of wood must be struck off. For instruments with more than three legs, care must be taken that all of them stand properly an the floor. This can be done either with the use of

wedges or, in the case of Neupert instruments, by means of an arrangement on the middle legs which permits one to compensate for irregularities in the floor. The lifting of the larger and heavier harpsichords requires at least three men, two on the sides, gripping the instrument from underneath in the area of the jack slides, the other at the tail.

3. In regard to the placement of the harpsichord in a room, the situation is not different from that of a piano; the harpsichord should not be close to an oven, heater (or heat outlet), nor window where air or sunlight could cause damage. The best place is near a dry interior wall or in the middle of a room. It should never be placed right up against a wall, since dampness is always present in walls that are thought to be quite dry; such dampness will cause trouble in the instrument. On the other hand, one should also avoid overheating (which is also bad for health in general) and the unnatural dryness of air that goes along with it; both of these are characteristic of central heating unless some means of introducing humidity into the air is provided. The average amount of humidity is about 70 per cent and in normally heated rooms (c. 72 F) it drops to about 55 per cent. It is for this degree of humidity that most artificially dried wood, with a moisture content of about 10 per cent, is intended. Excessive humidity will cause swelling, and excessive dryness, warping and splitting. The former may be obviated by using dry heat, the latter by introducing moisture into the air by some means (use of a humidifier at the rate of about four quarts of water more per day). Pianos and thus harpsichords as well as any other kind of furniture can stand continually overheated or underheated rooms or rapidly changing temperature no better than can human beings; man and instrument will react by impairment of health. Thus, as a general rule, the following should be observed: irregular and abnormal conditions of temperature and humidity and sharp changes in either or both are to be avoided as much as possible. If they are unavoidable, then time must be allowed for the instrument to settle down. This is especially true when the harpsichord is transported during the winter, when it is best to begin heating the room only after the harpsichord has been unpacked and its lid opened. If it is necessary to place it in an already heated room, the instrument should be left with its lid down for a few hours, since if it is opened too soon, its metal parts are likely to sweat and to rust, thus disturbing the action.

4. As already suggested, the ability of a harpsichord to stay in proper adjustment is closely related to external conditions and also to how often it is used and how much it is moved around. Definite rules on this cannot be established, but in evaluating the ability to stay in tune one should not forget that harpsichords made according to the strictest conditions have bracing of wood, a weak soundboard and make use of relatively weak strings (especially in the treble of the four foot register), which are far more delicate than those of a modern piano. It is not without reason that the harpsichord was regarded as a "sweet, but highly fickle instrument", something which modern techniques can probably improve, but cannot entirely do away with, because it is to some extent an inherent characteristic. Normally harpsichords are tuned to concert pitch (A = 435 to 440 vibrations per second), unless one wishes to do otherwise; at the same time they may be tuned a semitone lower without causing the tone quality to suffer and in this way can be made to approximate to the pitch level of the 18th century. Harpsichords should not be kept at a pitch very much higher than normal for long periods of time, since they are not built to stand this and their tone quality will quickly deteriorate. When new, harpsichords require frequent tuning, as is also the case with pianos, until a certain point of stability, which depends upon conditions where the instrument is kept, is reached and the strings have stretched to their proper length. The "ageing" process can be accelerated by occasionally tuning the instrument a semitone too high and leaving it standing for two or three days. This, however, should only be done to the uncovered steel strings. With harpsichords having more than three or four registers it should be done to two registers at first and only to the others when the first two have been retuned to their normal pitch, so that the frame and its supports will not have to suffer excessive pressure from the increased tension and pull of the strings. Tuning a semitone higher requires a 12 per cent increase in tension. Once the instrument is back at normal concert pitch, its ability to remain in tune will have improved noticeably.

Unused harpsichords should not be left untuned—this is bad economy. Tuning may be done by the harpsichordist himself if he has a good ear and knowledge of musical temperament and—what is more important— is familiar with the proper use of the tuning key. It is of particular importance in harpsichords—and this is something that must be made clear even to professional tuners—that the tuning pins are to be turned and not pressed, otherwise they will soon be quite useless. Only the tuning key supplied with the instrument should be used, so that the threading on the pins remains undamaged.

First of all the "a" of the eight foot register should be tuned according to a tuning fork or other means and then the others in accordance with the circle of fifths or any other procedure.[71] The first cycle (see the chart) works with fifths and octaves, the second with fifths and fourths. In the tempered scale, as opposed to the pure scale, the fifths must be tuned narrow (or flat), i. e. made smaller, the fourths wide (or sharp), i. e. made larger, while the octaves remain pure. For comparison and as a check, major thirds and sixths (the filled-in notes on the chart), which are noticeably larger than their pure counterparts in the scale, pure as well as triads and tenths, should be used. When the tempering is properly done in one full octave, one should then proceed from the middle range first by octaves down to the bass and then up through the treble, and similar checking is advisable here as well. A second eight foot register may be tuned to the first and others can be tuned from it in octaves. A tuning wedge is not necessary, thus making the process somewhat simpler than it is with the piano. Before turning a tuning pin one should first always make certain that one has the proper one by checking both pitch and register, since turning the wrong pin will result in breaking a string. If the factory has not already done so, one should mark certain tuning pins as guides (marking all the pins controlling "a" strings). Beyond errors made in tuning and other violent damage or through rust, one needs scarcely concern himself with the possibility of breaking a string, since in properly constructed instruments sufficient reserve strength is allowed for when the strings are designed.

---

[71] Recently electronic tone producers have been put on the market which give proper-pitches over a range of one or more octaves, such as the American "Stroboconn" and the device developed by Professor Feldkeller in Reutlingen, Germany. Such devices may be used in tuning a harpsichord. Another method of avoiding tuning by the cycle of fifths is to tune the instrument by an ordinary properly tuned table harmonium, like the Hohner organetta. This will be easier to do if one reduces the volume of the instrument to which the harpsichord is being tuned, by covering it or by drilling small holes that may be closed in its wind magazine.

5. Replacements for broken strings, since special wire is needed, must be obtained from the factory and one must supply the model designation, the register and pitch of all plain strings and for covered strings the pieces of the string themselves must be sent. If they are not available and the instrument does not have normal measurements, the following information should be supplied: the distance from the hitch pin to the soundboard bridge, the speaking length of the string from the soundboard bridge pin to the wrest plank bridge pin, as well as its register and pitch. In order to make the indication of the pitch absolutely unequivocal, it is suggested that the keys be counted from the lowest up or highest down, and this information also be given: so and so many strings from the bottom, as the case may be. But, as already been said, careful treatment and above all the avoidance of unnecessarily touching the strings with the hands or tools will make such replacements very rare indeed. As for the covered strings, faulty winding, dirt and other damage can cause them to become "dead", i. e., not capable of producing a full sound and thus they will need to be replaced.

The installation of new strings should be done in the following manner: as preparation, the remnants of the old string must be removed, together with all jacks in the immediate area, to avoid any possible damage to them. The new string is attached to the hitch pin by its loop, led across the bridges on the soundboard and wrest plank to a point about 2^{1}/$_{2}$ in. (6 cm) beyond the tuning pin. The tuning pin must be turned backwards 5 complete turns. Now the end of the string is inserted through the hole drilled in the tuning pin far enough so that its end is not projecting from the opposite side. This must naturally be done from right to left, so that the string will be made taut when the pin is turned clockwise.

Now, while turning the pin clockwise, the thumb of the left hand presses the string against the pin, so that under the combined effect of turning and pressing the string goes firmly into position and with further turning of the pin is forced flush against it. Here one must see to it that in the turning process the string is neatly wound around the pin, one wind next to the previous one, as can be seen from the other pins. The string is then slowly tuned higher with constant checking of pitch and one must again make certain that the string is properly secured at all points. A new string will not stay in tune very long at first, but will require frequent retuning until it has had time to stretch properly. The jack, too, will usually need some adjustment.

6. To make a harpsichord properly playable, together with tuning one must adjust the voicing of all the plectra within a register. On early instruments such regulating required considerable skill since one had to deal with fractions of millimeters, but on modern instruments it has been made quite easy by the use of finely threaded drop screws on the jacks. The jack rail, which covers all the jacks, is removed (it usually is locked in position by a bolt of some kind), the jacks needing adjustment are taken out of the jack guide carefully and adjusted with a screw driver supplied with the instrument (the use of a screw driver that does not fit quite exactly will destroy the fine slote and damage the jacks). To increase volume the screw is turned left (counter-clockwise), to decrease, to the right (clockwise). This applies whether the drop screw is on the upper half of the jack or the lower, but in the former case, quite common today, it is not necessary to remove the jack from the jack guide at all. A minute turn will suffice to produce considerable variation in the volume of tone. The weakness of the strings and frame used in early harpsichords should not lead one to voice modern instruments up too much—this will not make the tone any more noble. It is recommended that only one jack be removed at a time, so that they will not get mixed up; this possibility, however, is taken care of by numbering all the jacks within a register consecutively from left to right (bass to treble) and stamping this number together with an indication of the register on each jack.

On the Neupert "OK" metal jacks with their "silvertone" plectra this adjustment has been greatly simplified and the degree of precision of operation has been increased. Disturbances caused by climate are impossible on such jacks, which are made of a light metal coated with a chemical protecting cover and mounted in stainless steel. Furthermore, thanks to the thumbscrews located at the top, in making adjustments one does not need to use a screw driver, nor is it necessary to remove the jacks from the jack slide.

7. One can make use of the opportunity afforded by such voicing adjustments to check the mobility of the tongue and its spring, naturally without doing any forcing and only in accordance with its normal motion. Any repair of loose or tight centerpins (made necessary by extraneous noise or sticking of the tongues) should be left to a professional technician who will be acquainted with this through working with pianos. Any looseness or tightness in the jack's centerpin is a sign of excess humidity and will disappear by itself when the humidity is taken care of. Lesser degrees of stiffness can be overcome by adjusting the spring, slightly increasing the amount of pressure to the tongue. This is easy in the case of metal springs; with those made of hog's bristle, a narrow brush tip that has been warmed (not hot) should be gently applied to turn it more sharply against the tongue. Replacing of the jack should be done as carefully as its removal and care should be taken to see that its plectrum is properly aligned in relation to neighbouring jacks in the register.

8. If not only individual notes but a whole register is felt to be either too strong or too weak in volume, the entire register should be regulated by means of the capstan screws that control the sidewise motion of the jack slide. These screws can be found on the side of the jack slide facing the leather plectra of the jacks in the registers. If a capstan screw is turned further in, the volume will be increased; if it is unscrewed, the volume will be decreased. All this depends upon the location of this screw in relation to the slide itself. When the capstan screws are located on the sides of the instrument's frame on rods or bars, one must act accordingly. Any adjustment must be carefully checked by playing on the register in question, since often the most minute adjustment is all that is needed. Such an adjustment affecting an entire register through capstan screws will often require additional regulation of screws on individual jacks, which are the only means of bringing about that last degree of refine-

ment. If the register is equipped with a piano stop, this precise adjustment should be made with the piano stop operative, since experience has shown that adjustments made with piano stop operative, usually sound better, when returned to the forte-position than the other way around. Usually an adjustment on few individual jacks will be sufficient. When, however, a jack has been set back so often that no further change is possible, then the entire register must be moved by the capstan screw, thus making sufficient space once again available for individual adjustments.

9. Screws which control the return of the jack slide are also present on its other side; these are almost never in need of adjustment: only when, in spite of much regulating, individual jacks still pluck the strings slightly even though the register is slid off. To correct this, the capstan screw should be turned as little as is absolutely necessary to prevent this plucking, since too much would bring the jacks too close to neighbouring vibrating strings, a situation that would produce extraneous noise.

10. It can happen, if these capstan screws are adjusted too often, that none of the registration devices (pedals, knee-levers, etc.) will be any longer sufficient to move the jack slide into a proper position. To remedy this, these devices must be set back so that they need not move so far before commencing to be effective. This can be accomplished by means of screws located underneath the key bed. If, however, the stop works by pulling, the connecting bars must be made shorter; but, on the other hand, if it works by pressure, then they must be lengthened, which can be accomplished by means of a nut. The way these connecting rods run in any particular register can most easily be determined by moving the pedals or knee-levers and following the movement of the various parts. See fig. 6, schematic diagram of a harpsichord register slide mechanism, on page 85.

11. A few additional suggestions for the proper loudness adjustment of the various registers may be given here, even though this is a field where individual preferences, conditions prevailing where the instrument is kept, the purpose for which it is to be used, the other instruments that may be involved, etc., play a great role. Small harpsichords with one register should be adjusted to correspond to a mezzo forte; if there are two registers, one should be at mezzo forte, the other at piano, except where a piano stop is present to provide more variation. With two

94

manual instruments, the forte register is usually the one controlled by the lower manual, the piano by the upper; coupling then produces "volles Werk". In the case of the greatly favoured Bach disposition (eight and sixteen foot registers on the lower manual, eight and four foot registers on the upper), the eight foot register on the lower is thought of as basic and should be adjusted to mezzo forte. Historical evidence does not support a wide variation in dynamics, which do not really make the sound carry better and produce in addition extraneous noises, difficult action and the like. This applies also to the sixteen foot register, where a forte adjustment is particularly to be avoided, especially in the very low bass. The eight foot register of the upper manual should be piano, since it is often used to produce echo effects in contrast to the lower manual. The four foot register on the upper manual should be not too piano, at any rate louder than the eight foot register of the upper manual, so that when "volles Werk" is played it contributes a brightness to the overall sound.

The characteristics of the plectrum action are such that one should never fall into the practice of voicing the instrument too loud in the belief that this adjustment is necessary since "the harpsichord does not come through in ensemble playing, it cannot be heard among the other instruments", and the like. This is not the task of the harpsichord and the solution lies rather in using fewer players or in moderating the whole manner of performance.

12. Within such a basic adjustment, piano and lute stops provide more variety, the application of which must rest with the inclination and feeling of the individual harpsichordist. Additional refinements on the piano stops can offer still further variation. When the lute dampers are not movable, their effectiveness can be enhanced by loosening the felt somewhat with a needle. Too much pressure should be avoided, so that the vibration of the string will not be impeded, a danger that is significant with the shorter strings and which may be overcome by pressing the felt closer together.

13. The sounding of a tone after the key has been released can be eliminated by sliding the damper down, an operation controlled by a small screw, unless such sounding is caused by the jack not returning to

a position sufficiently low to damp the string. If this damper adjustment is insufficient, the capstan screw at the bottom of the jack should be screwed further in, thus permitting the jack to drop down more.

14. The real purpose of this capstan screw, however, is the regulation of the distance between the plectrum and the string. This adjustment is correct when in depressing the key there is about $3/32$ inch (2 mm) before the resistance caused by the contact between plectrum and string begins to be felt. A closer adjustment makes it difficult for the tongue on the jack to return to its orignal position when the key is released and the jack falls back. Anything greater than $3/32$ to $1/8$ of an inch (2 to 3 mm) has a bad effect on the action and, if several registers sound simultaneously, can cause the plucking action to cease altogether. These capstan screws also make possible the simultaneous plucking by several jacks controlled by the same key; these jacks are located between the strings and parallel to them. The best method to use here is to take an eight foot register that sounds properly by itself as the basis for the adjustment of the others, while the easiest is to adjust the slower of the two jacks. Where these capstan screws are lacking, as in the smaller flat instruments, the jacks may be filed down a little or their length increased by glueing small bits of paper to the bottoms. Since in normal playing a slight difference in timing is not noticeable, this adjustment will scarcely need to be made.

15. On the other hand, with wooden jacks the following happens quite frequently and is caused by climate, dust or other foreign particles: a jack sticks, either does not fall back upon release of the key or does not rise at all when the key is depressed. When this occurs, the jack should be removed from the jack slide and rubbed with the finest grade sandpaper at the points where it is sticking; such places are easily identifiable from the dark scratches, caused by metal oxide from the slide. These scratches are extremely small and only the slightest amount of sanding is needed to make the jack operate properly once again. There must not be a great deal of play between the jack and the jack slide if the intensity of the plucking is to remain uniform; this is especially important for instruments with a piano stop. If the sticking is slight it is often sufficient to press the key up and down several times while bearing down on the top of the jack with a finger, thus overcoming the resistance. If the sticking

is caused by humidity, the jack should be removed and subjected to a carefully controlled drying and warming process, either in the sun or through some artificial means (heaters or ovens). At all events the source of such excess humidity should also be eliminated. Any improper functioning of the jacks, such as sticking or slipping of any kind, is an indication of unfavourable conditions where the instrument is kept.

If metal jacks, which are tightly fitted into the jack guide, stick, this is generally caused by dust or, at times, sweating. In the former case the jack guide should be cleaned with the rounded brushes supplied with the instrument; in the latter, the jack itself must be cleaned with some alcoholic solvent (such as carbon tetrachloride or a nitrate solution), but chemicals of this sort should not be allowed to come in contact with either the plectrum or the damper. Lubricating oil should never be used, since in time it and the everpresent dust will combine to form a layer that would impede the action.

16. When the register stops fail to function, i. e. the jack slides do not move from left to right, or the spring mechanism fails to return them to their original position, the cause will more likely be found to lie in the sticking of the slides themselves than in the malfunctioning of the spring. The first of these can be remedied by increasing from front to back the area in which the slide operates, which can be done by removing the shims from both sides of the frame. Occasionally the sticking is caused by excessive pressure of the jack slide against the little cross-ledge; the cross-ledge screws should be loosened somewhat. The second and quite rare situation, caused by an ineffectual or broken register spring should be left to a repairer.

17. In general, repairs of keyboards, pedals and coupling, should be left to trained repair men, since such work usually calls for major dismantling of the instrument, for which professional knowledge and experience are necessary. If no such technician is available, or if no one familiar with harpsichords is at hand, it is best to seek advice from the factory before work of this kind is undertaken. For this one must supply an exact description of what seems wrong with the instrument: information on where the harpsichord is kept, how it is used, its previous treatment, etc., will often assist in determining the cause of the problem.

In regard to cleaning the interior of harpsichords (and keyboard instruments in general), a question which comes up all the time, it can be said that the best and least dangerous method is to use bellows or a vacuum cleaner. If this does not take care of an unduly large accumulation of dust on the soundboard, one can try carefully to guide a small duster with a flexible handle along the surface of the soundboard beneath the strings. A duster may also be used to clean the keys, moistened slightly with water or alcohol, mixed with water.

Rust on the strings and other metal parts at first effects only the appearance of the instrument, but eventually will cause significant damage and should be corrected. This means not only cleaning off the rust but also eliminating its cause (see no. 3). One should take a small piece of non-fibrous cloth or a soft piece of leather and gently rub the affected places. In extreme cases a piece of the finest steel wool may be employed. The change in the colour of the brass, silver and copper parts is not the result of rust, but is caused by natural oxydation. One is particularly warned against the use of lubricating oil for this, since if such oil is allowed to come in contact with the tuning pins the instrument will soon be totally ruined. The best protection against moths is to keep the instrument where it is light, well-ventilated and relatively free from dust and, as is necessary, to apply insect powder with care, but nothing liquid, since this should only be applied to the interior of a manual by a competent repairer.

18. The repair of more extensive damage, the replacement of broken jacks or other parts, and of the leather plectra, should be left to the factory or a good repair man. There is little value in obtaining such replacement parts from here and there, since with instruments of this kind all the various parts are carefully made in close relationship to one another and this process requires special tools. For this reason the part in question should be returned to the factory, where the needed work will be carried out and the part sent back as soon as possible.

Small cracks in the soundboard, which can occur in spite of the most careful drying of the wood, particularly in the winter when it is cold and dry, have no effect on the operation and sound of the instrument, except when they on occasion can cause extraneous noise. If such cracks do not close of themselves during the humid season, they can be pressed together by a skilled repair man. The cracking of the lacquer coating of the soundboard, which occurs in very cold weather, has no more effect on wood than it has on porcelain.

Generally in cases of doubt one should seek advice from the factory, whose staff has had experience over several decades. This will save the instruments from damage caused by ignorant treatment.

At first reading these suggestions may seem a little confusing and even frightening, but one should remember that there it was necessary to take care of all possible eventualities, so that the layman as well as the technician will find some basis for "first aid". One should use them as a means of obtaining a clear and detailed understanding of the way the plectrum action operates; an understanding of the rest will come by making a careful study of the instrument itself.

19. In conclusion, a few remarks on playing the harpsichord. The plectrum action requires a precise attack, clean fingering, no use at all of weight in playing; controlled posture, keeping the arms light, the fingers striking quickly and moving from the third joint, resting lightly on the keys, and making careful legato connections from note to note — these are the secrets of classical harpsichord technique. [72] Great effort in attack is not needed, even when there is no manual coupling, since the force with which the keys are struck has almost no influence on volume and when overdone can cause extraneous noise from the instrument. [73] It is

---

[72] An extensive discussion of this subject is found in Harich-Schneider: *Die Kunst des Cembalospiels* (Kassel, 1939), or its shortened English edition, The Harpsichord, An Introduction to Technique, Style and the Historical Sources (Kassel and St. Louis, 1954). A short summary of important aspects in harpsichord playing is given in Bittner: "Versuchung zum Cembalospiel", *Deutsche Musikkultur,* III (1939, no. 6), 442–455. Also, M. F. Schneider: *Beiträge zu einer Anleitung Clavichord und Cembalo zu spielen* (Strassburg, 1934). Further, reference may be made to Harich-Schneider: *Kleine Schule des Cembalospiels* (Kassel, 1952).
Interesting questions relating to the differentiation between the piano and the harpsichord styles in conjunction with contemporary music have been treated by Franz-peter Goebels, who is both harpsichordist and pianist in articles such as "Cembalo und Klavier in der Gegenwart," *Musikleben,* VII (1954) and "Neue Musik für Tasten-instrumente," *Hausmusik,* XVIII (1954).
[73] The force necessary to apply to the front of the key to produce the plucking has been established at between 50 and 380 grams (the variations depending upon the manual and registration involved) through tests made on the so-called Bach-Flügel; see Tetzel: "Der Anschlag beim Klavierspiel in mechanischer und physiologischer Hinsicht," *Zeitschrift für Musikwissenschaft,* X (1928), 30 f.

necessary only that the plucking takes place cleanly and with rhythmic precision. With regard to the "feel" of playing a harpsichord, it is close to that of tracker organ. As in organ playing where the air pressure in the valve must be overcome, so in the harpsichord there is a point where the string's resistance is broken and hence an exact moment at which the sound is produced. Lifting the finger once the key is allowed to return must not be delayed, since the tongue should not remain too long in the immediate neighbourhood of the vibrating string. The operation of register stops and pedals should also be definite and precise. The method of operating here is generally positive-pulling or pressing the stop slides the register into sounding position; in instruments containing more than three pedals, the pedals may be locked in the position by a lateral motion. One should accustom one's self to operating the pedals quietly and by feel (without looking), leaving the foot in contact with the pedal until it has been returned to its rest position, so that no excess noise is produced.

The use of the various registers is determined by the character of the music to be played and the interpretation of the performer. The same is true of tempo, but one is emphatically warned against playing too fast. The strings need a certain amount of time to be able to produce a cantabile sound and playing too fast detracts from the essential fine points of harpsichord tone, its clarity and cleanness, making everything obscure and confused. The tempo is correct when the work is given full value both as a whole and in its individual parts. The performance of early music must be based on a strict adherence to the tempo once it has been established.

Before making a public appearance the harpsichordist should become familiar with all tonal combinations and technical qualities of the instrument. The harpsichord is an "incorruptible instrument, an instrument with character", as Harich-Schneider (op. cit.) puts it: "It appears splendid and magnificent in 'volles Werk' when properly treated, or so resisting when not. A wrong note on the piano is nothing very serious —but one on the harpsichord is like spilled ink. And nothing sounds as awful, as dry and repelling, as a harpsichord played with a faulty touch."

Recently developed technical methods have permitted to incorporate into the modern harpsichord many improvements which have no influence on the tone of the instrument, so that any player is able to do what is recommended by a contemporary harpsichordist [74] in the treatment of the instrument: "Before each concert he should check his registers and the uniformity within a register, the relation between the registers carefully, particularly the dynamic level of the various eight foot registers; the instrument should never be adjusted so that it sounds too loud, since its tone will lose clarity; the instrument will make too much noise, the listener will be unable to distinguish, and clarity is the most important thing. A harpsichordist playing a flawless instrument will alone be in a position to accomplish something of lasting value towards the harpsichord renaissance and thus to produce an art full of animation and the affirmation of life."

---

[74] M. Kastner: "Die heutige Cembalokunst", *Die Musik* (1932, no. 1).

POSTSCRIPT TO THE FOURTH GERMAN EDITION (1966)

It is always pleasurable and gratifying for an author, when a new edition of his work is called for. As the present monograph on the harpsichord has always, ever since its conception in 1932, been intended by the author primarily as a handbook for harpsichord owners, to give them guidance as to the origin, type and maintenance of the instrument, there seemed no reason to make any changes in the second and third edition. It was a matter for careful consideration, whether to bring out a fourth, phototype, edition, a method which would allow, as you know, very little alteration of the text.

For indeed, in the intervening period of more than thirty years, the harpsichord movement, and harpsichord making, have not stood still. In the last ten years, in particular, three important publications in English have appeared, dealing with the harpsichord: Boalch's book, "Makers of the Harpsichord and Clavichord, 1440—1840", gives details of more than 820 makers, and more than 1,000 historical instruments; Russell's book "The Harpsichord and Clavichord" is especially valuable for its exposition of the various historical branches in harpsichord building by the addition of extensive appendices of original sources; and finally Hubbard's book "Three Centuries of Harpsichord making" is outstanding, both as a study of the characteristics and methods of the five main schools of harpsichord making (Italy, Netherlands, France, England, Germany) and for its appendix of translated sources and numerous diagrams.

Full of information and interest as these works are to the specialist and musicologist, there still seems to be a place for the present handbook, with its more modest pretensions; but it is true that it needed to be brought up to date. Publisher and author together saw the opportunity of doing this for the phototype edition, by the inclusion of the following lecture, delivered by the author to the Galpin Society in London in 1962, and also on the occasion of the first Europiano Congress in Berlin in 1965. In this lecture an account was rendered of what has been going on in German harpsichord making in the last decade, what new ideas and productions have been circulating until now. For this reason it is inevitable that some of the subject matter, particularly under the heading "Modern Reconstruction" is repeated. Some of the ideas of 1932 are still valid theses to-day. Others have developed into subjects of controversy, as my lecture will now show!

SOME PRESENT DAY PROBLEMS CONNECTED WITH THE HARPSICHORD AND HARPSICHORD MAKING
(Translation by Ann P. P. Feldberg)

I intend to give only a little time to the problems, in order to give much more, instead, to controversial matters connected with the subject, for you must remember, harpsichord making was carried on from about the 15th century up to 1800, and then again from 1888; that is, for about four centuries in the earlier period, and then for a further eighty years up to the present time. If by "problems" we mean "unsolved difficulties", it would be a rather poor outlook if, in a limited field, such as harpsichord making, the experts had achieved so little in five centuries that there were still many problems to solve. They have concerned themselves, both in former times, and now in making new harpsichords, with all the various technical possibilities, in various ways, and have found the necessary solutions, with the result that the harpsichord is once again able to flourish in our time.

Especially in Germany, the production of harpsichords has reached a notable figure, of value about DM 5 million at a conservative estimate; a high proportion is for export, and the annual production is higher than the total number of instruments made by many historical workshops in their whole lifetime. Admittedly these are only bald figures, but they seem to me to confirm that:

a) There is very strong interest in modern harpsichords and that

b) Modern harpsichord makers can hardly be entirely on the wrong lines.

We are charged with this latter point, indeed, by many of our critics, who gain a hearing in works specialising in instrument building, musical periodicals, concert notices and recently occasionally on gramophone record sleeves. From these criticisms one or two points of controversy have emerged, and I would like to discuss these now: —

I hope you will excuse me if I am not able to remain entirely objective, but a clean division between the subject and the man is really very difficult in my case, since harpsichord making, both in the written and the spoken word, and above all in practice, has been my profession and life's work. And I shall have to explain, and to vindicate, some things in which I have myself been largely involved.

This sentence was written a few years ago in an accepted English work on the harpsichord: that present day harpsichord building is in a "state of adolescence and (I hope) of change". When we consider that modern harpsichord building started in 1888 and think of the advances that the experts have made during that time, as I know from my own experience—we can hardly take the first part of this statement seriously.

As for the second part, that harpsichord building is in "a state of change", I can, as participant, agree wholeheartedly here, for such a condition seems to me to afford an especially stimulating atmosphere for our branch of work. Is it not gratifying and pleasurable that, even though one is pursuing an historical subject, one can keep moving, progressing, and even expanding, as harpsichord maker to-day? This is no narrow-minded, „history-bound" matter, and one must not devote oneself, as harpsichord maker, solely to copying.

Nowadays reproductions or meticulously accurate copies of original instruments, which were general at the beginning of the revival, are only ordered and made for some particular scientific or artistic purpose. This is an intellectually cheap, technically fussy, and in g e n e r a l use, an unsatisfactory method, on which I have commented already in my lecture "Copy and Reconstruction" on the occaison of the International Musicological Congress 1953. Just as Dolmetsch in England rejected the system of reproducing old instruments ("the masters did not copy one another"), so for the most part the German harpsichord makers have decided in favour of "reconstruction", proclaiming with Faust that "in marching forward there is both torment and happiness".

As I see it, "reconstruction" is freely to recreate the old keyboard instruments out of our own imagination, so that they offer to modern people the original acoustical characteristics of these instruments. For this purpose the old instruments should be studied, in order to discover their qualities of permanent value. They should not, however, act as a curb on any chance advances in technology. The old instruments were so various and so devoid of any rigid standardisation, that we too may well assume the right to make for the over-riding and constant aim of true harpsichord tone by any appropriate means known to us at the present day. In saying this I am not bowing down at the feet of technical innovation, but I am making my defence against the type of criticism that takes for its text "wrong because it's new!"

The historic old masters are in no way dishonoured if we make use of new developments in acoustics, statics, mechanics, technology and production methods. After all, our customers are not period people of the seventeenth and eighteenth centuries, but citizens of our own time in their behaviour, their reactions, their attitudes and their demands.

Modern man surrounded by precision work and technical skill can no longer accept the inevitable idiosyncrasies of the old instruments and their copies with the patience and resignation of the "Kenner und Liebhaber" of earlier centuries, specially as he has not, on the whole, the familiarity with their musical mechanics that was previously taken for granted. He demands, therefore, at least a rational approach to the mechanical side of the instrument. Deficiencies in the action lead rather to a falling off in the use of the instrument than to that wider circulation, which we would wish to see for every musical instrument, as something in everyday use.

The responsible harpsichord maker, indeed, makes no changes merely for the sake of joy in the experiment, but only because he wants to improve acknowledged weaknesses in the older instruments; he wants to make them easier to play, or more versatile, or simpler to maintain. The modern harpsichord has changed from the old, only for this reason.

The difference between the old methods of building and our own becomes apparent as soon as one looks at the wooden back, or main frame, of the larger models. In the old instruments the case was simply a box. The side walls had to withstand the strain of the string tension in spite of their frailty. In the instruments of the Italian School they were reinforced only by small wooden buttresses; the Flemish and French Schools used crossbarring on the base plate. The English School, of Broadwood and Kirckman, was already employing a sounder system for bracing the structure, which led to the change to the methods we favour nowadays, at least in the larger instruments. This consists of two separate components, the back, the skeleton of the instrument, and the casework glued to this afterwards.

Instruments built in this way are certainly somewhat heavier, but no-one would deny their greater stability and the favourable effect this has on their ability to hold their tuning and to resist warping under stress. Only those who have never had to tackle the task of putting an original instrument, too lightly built for stability, extremely infirm and distorted, into playing order, keeping it in tune and mechanically viable, can possibly deny the importance of stability.

Opponents of this type of construction (i. e. the modern type), maintain that it interferes with the free vibrations of the strings. They overlook the fact that neither the case nor the frame is involved in this function. Now, as then, it is the soundboard which is responsible for taking up the string vibrations, which are passed to it through the soundboard bridges. Because the soundboard is so vital, it cannot be considered a failing to employ proved methods of choice of wood, seasoning, barring and laminating, taken over from piano building — a field where the soundboard has been the subject of numerous experiments and patents. Of course, for the harpsichord maker there is the additional problem of adapting what he borrows from piano making to the slighter proportions of the harpsichord, but the aim in both is the same: to create out of wood a light, uniformly vibrating membrane of permanent elasticity.

Hence we find that the closed case has no significant effect on the tone of the larger instruments, but, on the contrary, its strength and carrying power is increased because of the open under side of the soundboard.

A little while ago, in order to take the wind from the sails of those uncompromising champions of the box type of harpsichord making, we developed and patented on two models a system for the acoustic layout, which provides adequate bracing for the box construction, but has an independent free-vibrating case, with a special gap between the two, resulting in a combination of the acoustical characteristics of the historical method of construction with the statical advantages of modern technique.

There have been many changes in the action, when compared to the old methods. These changes effect materials, shape, guiding and regulating mechanisms, but not the working principle of the quill activating the string by plucking. It is true that some attempts have been made at harpsichord substitute instruments, but they do not come within the scope of our present discussion.

Jacks were usually made of wood, but this has the unsuitable property of being hygroscopic. The jack guides were of the same material. If the jacks were a close fit in the guides, dampness would cause swelling and jamming. If they were allowed more tolerance, the loose-fitting jack would give uneven regulation. The first remedy to be tried was the metal jack rack. The next step was to impregnate the wood, or to give a firm guide to the attacking side of the jack, while it rested against a weak spring on the other side. Finally, plastic, as specially perfected by the chemist, largely superseded wood as jack material, rather than one of the other substitute materials. It proves itself adaptable, easy to work, and impervious to all external conditions.

We can get an almost higher degree of precision with these jacks than with a further development, the metal cylindrical jacks. The jack racks for these are light metal, with the cylindrically bored guide holes ringed with plastic washers to eliminate noise. With these most recent jacks (plastic and metal) we have taken our efforts a step further to make easier still the most important adjustment, that of the volume. Now the player need no longer remove the jack from the rack, but adjusts either the regulating screw at the top of the jack with a small screwdriver, or with his own two fingers.

Another part that is usually adjustable nowadays is the damper, attached to the jack—overhead damping is no longer used—which consists now of a wide damper felt, not a narrow strip of cloth as previously. This type of damping is more effective even if I am not altogether in favour of it from a musical point of view, since as a result we have to sacrifice part of the lingering resonance characteristic of old instruments. But modern players demand technical perfection above all, here and in other matters; in their choice of plectra material for jacks, for example.

Whether quill or leather was originally used on the old instruments, or whichever may have been used most, the modern harpsichord maker must have a material suitable for plucking, homogenous and durable. This has meant the eclipse of bird quill, and leather, oak-cured in tanning pits in the ancient manner, offers itself as a substitute. We are now so skilled in treating this that there is practically no difference in the tone. But here too plastic is already being used instead of leather, cylindrical-, conical- and prism-shaped. This comes nearer to the natural quill, and has the advantage, as a material, of being homogenous and easily replaced. If asked for my own opinion, I would say that leather is more congenial because of its warmer tone and its adaptability to different ways of cutting. In its turn, the sharper, cooler sound of plastic quill is very suitable for the 4' and 8' nazard. This means that in practice the choice is open to the maker and not least—the customer!

Then we have to decide whether we are going to equip modern harpsichords with hand stops, knee levers, slides or pedals. Any of these, and even combinations of several, can be used nowadays without any technical difficulty, so one can have, for example, the registers operated by pedals, and the effects (Harp, Piano) by hand stops. Usually we have only convenience to consider. It is incorrect when our critics say "In modern harpsichords the movement is usually controlled by pedals". The error arises from the fact that they do not know harpsichord making in its full range and all its various branches, because on the whole they form their opinions only on *concert harpsichords* which they see and hear whether in concerts, on disc or on tape. I do not think it sound to draw general conclusions about tendencies in construction and layout, from a few instruments specially designed for a particular purpose; for actually these make up only quite a small proportion of the total production today. It seems, from enquiries to the four largest German harpsichord workshops, that the proportion is between 10% and 17%, and will certainly not go higher in countries where the harpsichord has once more become an instrument for domestic and chamber music.

Furthermore, 5/6 of the total production, that is, the single manual instruments with one or two registers, and most of the two manual instruments with three registers, are not fitted with pedals. The remaining minority, about 1/6, the large instruments, are usually operated by pedals, since this amenity is almost always welcomed especially by concert players. In my opinion, the player must be responsible for possible misuse of the device through over-registering, just as it is the driver and not the car-factory who is responsible for speeding.

For practical reasons, a sort of common practice in the arrangement of the pedals has grown up among German makers; pedals to bring on the registers are on the outside, right and left; mechanical modifications, such as coupler or harp stops, are in the middle. All the same, some sort of international standardisation, as suggested by Mr Thurston Dart in a discussion at the Royal Musical Association in 1956, would be welcome.

Another common practice, although not exactly standardised, has emerged in Germany concerning keyboards, which are still made in specialist workshops to individual specifications. A keyboard of five octaves is 81 cm. wide; this is an average width based on a great number of historical instruments of the 18th century, and roughly corresponds to the measurements of Silbermann and Stein.

We come now to the subject of harpsichord dispositions, an ever recurring controversy, just as it is in the allied art of organ building. In this connection, it is pleasant to reflect that with the maximum of usually two manuals and four to five registers on the harpsichord, proportionally fewer combinations, and therefore problems, result. Countless experiments with dispositions have been made in the 80 years of modern harpsichord making, sometimes at the instigation of artists and musicologists, sometimes on the makers' own initiative. I can assure you that I have built more than forty different models myself, of which almost 7,000 examples have been made. About eight models survive in the current range, excluding copies and special orders. In general, I can say for modern German harpsichord making, that the problem of disposition has been as successfully solved as I declared in the first edition of my harpsichord monograph in 1933: "We are once more building all those dispositions which appeared in the original instruments as the most outstanding of their time". This holds good for spinets with 8', single manual harpsichords with 2 × 8' or 1 × 8' + 1 × 4', two manual harpsichords with 1 × 8' + 1 × 4' on the lower manual and 1 × 8' on the upper manual, with the additional possibilities of the 4' on the upper manual as well, by means of the shift coupler, and also the further use of the upper 8′ as lute stop, by means of a fourth row of jacks near the nut.

You will have noticed that all these dispositions are *without 16′*, and with the 4′ *on the lower manual*, so that the statement that the 16′ "is common in modern harpsichords" and "the 4′ is always on the upper manual" is just not true of German harpsichord making to-day, and probably no more true of other countries. The statement concerning the 16′ applies only to the first forty years of the harpsichord movement, when the pioneer harpsichord makers were concerned to make powerful concert harpsichords at all costs, which could appear side by side with the mighty concert grand pianos with some hope of success. The usual disposition at that time was 8′, 4′ and 16′ on the lower manual, 8′ on the upper manual used twice, that is, five rows of jacks in all with coupling possibilities. Most of these instruments had iron frames, and were very heavily strung, with tough leather plectra. To-day the metal frame has been abandoned (with exception, to my knowledge, in U.S.A.) and of necessity the stringing has had to be adapted to the weaker resistance of the wooden frame.

In about 1920 the predominance of this Pleyel-Landowska disposition for—I emphasize—large concert instruments, gave way to a disposition which is associated with Harpsichord no. 316 of the State Collection of Musical Instruments in Berlin, the ominous, formerly so-called "Bach Harpsichord": 8′, 16′ on the lower manual; 4′, 8′ on the upper manual, four rows of jacks, coupler. This instrument was held in the highest esteem for the first quarter of the century, until in 1924 Kinsky put on record his doubts as to J. S. Bach's ownership, and this viewpoint was later supported by the works of Kreichgauer (1938) and Ernst (1955). As time has gone on, the instrument has been more and more criticised — I might even say, torn to shreds. This was largely because it did not remain an isolated example; for most large harpsichord firms, and by no means only German ones, took it as a pattern for the layout and disposition of their concert harpsichords. Without specially defending this step, let me try to explain it to you, for I have followed this matter closely. Was there any reason to doubt this harpsichord's authenticity at that time, when musicologists like Spitta, Fleischer and above all Curt Sachs—

in his official catalogue of the collection in 1922 and in his little history of the piano in 1923—and again Galpin in 1937, in *European Musical Instruments*, referred to it as Johann Sebastian Bach's harpsichord? It was copied by Georg Steingraeber, Carl Pfeiffer, and Arnold Dolmetsch in collaboration with Gaveau, and was praised for its "majestic, resounding, historical tone" by the foremost harpsichord experts. If the musicologists themselves could not agree, is it to be wondered at, that this instrument became the prototype of the most popular concert harpsichords of the last forty years?

In fact, supposing this harpsichord had no direct connection with J. S. Bach, what is there to be said against it? Only that its disposition is different from nearly all the others, "is, in fact, unique". According to comparisons made by Mr Raymond Russell, it is similar to the few surviving large harpsichords of the well known and distinguished school of Hass in Hamburg. I do not believe that the existing 16' is a later addition, taking the place of an earlier third register at 8'; even the stringing wire of to-day could not stand up to the scaling of approximately 28 cm. in the treble. Knowing what delight the eighteenth century harpsichord maker found in experimenting, I can only think that this disposition was used with full knowledge and intent. I think that it never achieved any historical significance for the sole reason that the heyday of the harpsichord was coming to an end. We cannot prove this now, but in any case it is a demonstrable fact, that in the last thirty five years this particular disposition has been built, sold and played by the hundred, in innumerable concerts, on records and tape, by artists whose experience and authority in the interpretation of old music we would not wish to gainsay, by designating their chosen model as false. In its success lies its justification.

Even if it is not entirely satisfactory for technical reasons, it is at least an all-round instrument, which is much in demand to-day. One could count on the fingers of one hand the occasions when a special harpsichord is available for a particular style of music, but every concert programme shows how much one instrument is expected to accomplish.

I hope you will excuse me, if I seem very much in favour of this model, although it constitutes only the smallest part of the total production.

Increasing use of harpsichords and spinets as domestic instruments, has put the emphasis on the small and medium-sized instruments, (over 85% of the total), without 16' and with the 4' always on the lower manual; and for years now the larger harpsichords have also been made with this disposition. The fact that modern harpsichord making has not insisted on retaining certain old standard sizes, but has adapted its measurements to the often restricted room space of to-day, has contributed to the rise of the harpsichord as a domestic instrument. The strong demand for domestic models has proved us right, even if there have been attempts in certain quarters to discredit them with the expression "bijou".

The "Cembalino" was one attempt in this direction. This is a redevelopment of the clavicytherium, shaped like a small, elegant upright piano, but with a new vertical type of quill action. Indeed, the large harpsichord firms are so advanced in their constructive capacity, equipment and production organisation that they can satisfy every reasonable requirement of their customers extremely efficiently, at reasonable prices. However, this too displeases our critics, and they call modern harpsichords (as appears on a record sleeve) "Commercial goods". Well, and do you think that the Ruckers family worked solely for joy in their labour, and to the glory of God? No, they wanted to sell their instruments, and, as we know, not cheaply either!

When an article becomes a saleable commodity, it is the purchaser who determines the value, in the last resort, whether it is a harpsichord for an artist, a scholar or the retiring amateur and domestic music-maker. But I admit that its development can and should be guided too by research and technology.

To demonstrate, however, that modern harpsichord making does not favour new methods for their own sake I would like to give you an example from our own recent experience:

A few years ago (in 1960) after a number of experiments, a Swiss watch technician succeeded in taking out a patent for an invention, which makes it possible to influence the volume of harpsichord tone, piano or forte, through varying the force of the touch on the key. This he achieved by a development of our cylindrical metal jacks, using their natural physical inertia, and so realised, while retaining the plectrum action, Cristofori's "Gravicembalo col piano e forte". 250 years ago such an invention would have been revolutionary and would have affected musical composition and performance—especially as the action works perfectly, as we have proved with a test instrument.

But as the introduction of such a harpsichord, with unterraced crescendo effect, seemed to us ill-advised and generally dangerous, we laid the patent aside. The opinion of about thirty prominent musicologists, instrumental experts and concert musicians, obtained from a written enquiry, supported our decision overwhelmingly. Perhaps we may proceed with it later, when some music has been written for a harpsichord capable of such gradations of tone. That is a problem for the future.

In conclusion, one pressing problem must be mentioned, that of the audibility of the harpsichord in concert use. With ever larger concert halls, fuller orchestration and increasingly powerful tone from other instruments, and with the human threshold of hearing doubtless rising under the strain of the everlasting din of to-day—the normal concert harpsichord is frequently not found loud enough. Attempts to make the harpsichord louder mechanically, using large instruments with as many sounding registers as possible, very heavily strung and coarsely plucked, are not satisfactory either for the tone or the touch. Therefore we first experimented with electrical amplification with Prof. Trautwein in 1936 at the Berlin Olympiad. It is true that some harpsichord players in particularly large halls, sometimes made use of the existing loudspeaker system in the hall, placing a microphone beside the harpsichord. But none of these attempts was ever really succesful, being too complicated or too expensive. In addition, the harpsichord as the source of the sound was more or less drowned, or its tone seriously distorted—and after all, preserving the original harpsichord tone constitutes the real problem of amplification.

The problem seems now to have been solved by an invention of the Hungarian harpsichord player, Prof. Gát, which has been developed to concert standard, with friendly scientific support, through the Institut für Studiotechnik at the TU, Berlin. Through the most modern methods of electronics and transistor technique, the concert harpsichord now has at its disposal that reserve of tone, which it must have in modern conditions, if it is not to be overwhelmed, slowly but surely. Whether, and how, the player will use the amplification it is left for him to decide, without any technical compulsion. He has before him, in all respects of layout, playing technique and action, a perfectly normal concert harpsichord. We hope that we may have made a musically justifiable contribution to enable the harpsichord to stand up to modern concert life.

I hope that you have been able to gather from this talk that modern harpsichord making is still developing, and that it does not exclude from its programme the possibility of further technical advance, in spite of its strong ties with historical precedent. Please do not judge some of these innovations too hard from the historical point of view, but bear in mind that musical instruments should be alive to the people of their own time. Otherwise, a dead weight of history lurks in the background, that can smother the life out of them.

Let me finish with a quotation from Dr. Faustus, by Thomas Mann:

> "We cannot understand the new and young, if we are not at home with tradition. In the same way, our reverence for the old will be unreal and barren if we deny the new, which has developed from the old, of historical necessity."

This lecture, given by the present author, was followed by two other lectures. The first speaker of these two spoke as an adherent of the totally historical view, and paid homage almost solely to the Netherlands School. The second speaker (Harpsichord Maker Sassmann) corrected this onesided view and declared that one can and should tread different paths, as in fact is generally the case with German harpsichord making.

It is worth noting that similar dissensions have beset organ builders recently.

Just as in their case one is warned against an "over-refinement," that hesitates delicately over the question as to whether something "was there" before 1750, and just as they regard organic growth as essential, so is it just as vital for harpsichord making to shun the "flight from to-day." Let us view the harpsichord movement and harpsichord making as a tree, with one common trunk, but with many different branches. May the future show which branch is lacking in sap, and which finally bears the best fruit!

BIBLIOGRAPHY OF THE HISTORY
OF KEYBOARD INSTRUMENTS

Adlung, J., *Musica Mechanica Organoedi* (Berlin, 1768; facsm. reprint, ed. C. Mahrenholz, Kassel, 1931)

Bie, O., *Klavier, Orgel und Harmonium* (Leipzig, 1910)

Beijnum, B. van, *Bouw en Geschiedenis van het Klavier* (Rotterdam, 1932)

Boalch, D. H., *Makers of the Harpsichord and Clavichord to 1840* (London, 1956)

Closson, E., *Histoire du piano* (Brussels, 1944)

Dufourcq, N., *Le clavecin* (Paris, 1949)

Harding, R. E. M., *The Pianoforte* (Cambridge, 1933)

Hipkins, A. J., *A Description and History of the Pianoforte and the Older Keyboard Stringed Instruments* (London, 1896)

Hirt., F. J., *Meisterwerke des Klavierbaus* (Olten, 1955)

James, P., *Early Keyboard Instruments* (London, 1930)

Junghanns, H., *Der Piano- und Flügelbau* (Leipzig, 1932)

Kenyon, M., *Harpsichord Music. A Survey of the Virginals, Spinet and Harpsichord* (London, 1949)

Kinsky, G., *Katalog des musikhistorischen Museums von Wilhelm Heyer* (Cologne, 1910)

Krebs, K., "Die besaiteten Klavierinstrumente bis zum Anfang des 17. Jahrhunderts," *Vierteljahrsschrift für Musikwissenschaft*, VIII (1892)

Kropp, E. A., *Das Zupfklavier* (Berlin diss., 1925)

Neupert, H., "Cembalo," in *Die Musik in Geschichte und Gegenwart*, ed. F. Blume, II (Kassel, 1952)

Neupert, H., *Vom Musikstab zum modernen Klavier* (Bamberg, 1926)

Neupert, H., *Das Klavichord. Geschichte und technische Betrachtung des "eigentlichen Claviers"* (Kassel, ²/1956). Engl. Ausgabe *The Clavichord* (Kassel, 1965)

Norlind, T., *Systematik der Saiteninstrumente*, 2 vols. (Hannover, 1936–1939)

Paul, O., *Geschichte des Claviers* (Leipzig, 1868)

Praetorius, M., *Syntagma musicum*, II (Wolfenbüttel, 1618–1620; facsm. reprint, ed. W. Gurlitt, Kassel, 1929)

116

Rimbault, E. F., *The Pianoforte: its Origin, Progress and Construction* (London, 1860)

Russell, R., *The Harpsichord and Clavichord. An Introductory Study* (London, 1959)

Sachs, C., *Reallexikon der Musikinstrumente* (Berlin, 1913)

Sachs, C., *Handbuch der Musikinstrumentenkunde* (Leipzig, 1920)

Sachs, C., *History of Musical Instruments* (New York, 1940)

Sachs, C., *Das Klavier* (Berlin, 1923)

Schmitz, E., *Klavier, Klaviermusik und Klavierspiel* (Leipzig, 1919)

Spielmann, H., *Vom Klavier* (Cologne-Krefeld, 1951)

Virdung, S., *Musica getutscht und aussgezogen* (Basel, 1511; facsm. reprint, ed. L. Schrade, Kassel, 1931)

Wörsching, J., *Die historischen Saitenklaviere und der moderne Clavichord- und Cembalobau* (Mainz, 1946).

New publications

A. Baines, *Musical Instruments through the Ages*, Harmondsworth 1961, dto. deutsch: *Musikinstrumente*, München 1962.

D. Boalch, *Makers of the Harpsichord and Clavichord 1440–1840*, London 1956.

F. Hubbard, *Three Centuries of Harpsichord Making*, Cambridge/USA 1965.

S. Marcuse, *Musical Instruments, A Comprehensive Dictionary*, New York 1964.

R. Russell, *The Harpsichord and Clavichord, An Introductory Study*, London 1959.

R. Schulze, *How to Build a Baroque Concert Harpsichord*, New York 1954.

ILLUSTRATIONS

Plates

1. Psaltery player from the frescoes of Orcagna in Camposanta at Pisa

Dulcimer and psaltery (Neupert Museum of Music History)

3. Above:
Earliest pictorial representation of a harpsichord in the Weimarer Wunderbuch (c. 1440) (Großherzogliche Bibliothek, Weimar)

Spinetten Virginal (in gemein Instrument genant) so recht Chor-Ton. 3 Octav Instrumentlin.

4. Below:
Spinet, virginal and spinettino (after Praetorius)

5. Above:
Oldest extant harpsichord, made by Hieronymus Bononiensis, Rome, 1521 (Victoria and Albert Museum, London)

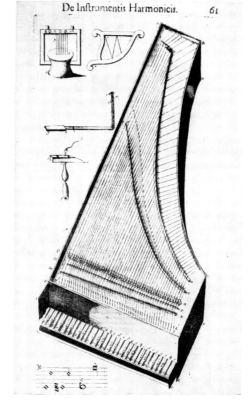

De Inftrumentis Harmonicis.   61

6. Below:
Drawing of a harpsichord with registers at four and eight foot pitch (according to Mersenne, 1635) along with early psalteries, plectrum action and tuning hammer

7. H. Ruckers virginal, Antwerp, 1610 (Händelhaus in Halle, Saxony)

8. Spinet by J. H. Silbermann, Straßburg, 1767 (Neupert Museum of Music History)

9. Italian spinet, 1673 (Neupert Museum of Music History)

V

10. Italian harpsichord made by Baffo, Venice, 1581
(Neupert Museum of Music History)

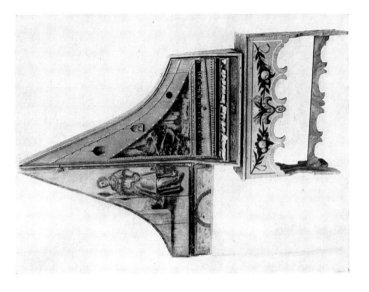

12. Earliest clavicytherium from Northern Italy, second half of the 15th century (Donaldson Museum, London)

11. Title page of Parthenia (London, 1611)

13. Italian spinettino with short octave, made around 1700 (Neupert Museum of Music History)

14. Two manual "Bachflügel" (Staatl. Instrumentensammlung, Berlin)

15. Two manual harpsichord made by A. Ruckers, Antwerp, 1617
(Neupert Museum of Music History)

16. Harpsichord by Johann Daniel Dulcken, Antwerp, 1689
(Neupert Museum of Music History)

17. Three manual harpsichord by B. Cristofori, Florence, 1703
(Neupert Museum of Music History)

18. Italian harpsichord, first half of the 18th century

19. Modern two manual harpsichord in the Ruckers disposition
(Neupert, Bamberg)

20. Modern spinet
(Neupert, Bamberg)

21. Modern spinettino
and its case
(Neupert, Bamberg)

22. Modern two manual harpsichord in the Bach disposition with pedal harpsichord
(Neupert, Bamberg)

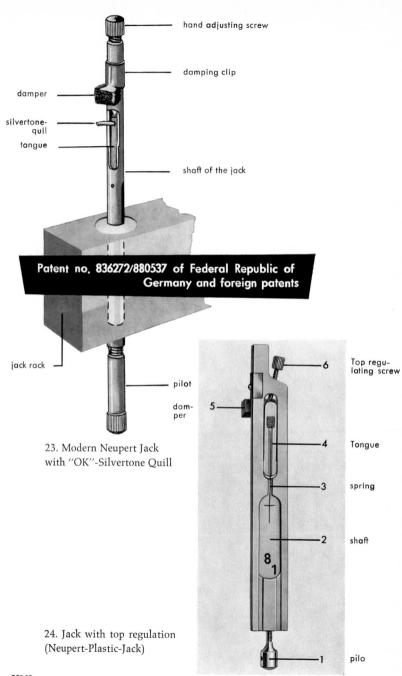

hand adjusting screw

damping clip

damper

silvertone-
qui!

tongue

shaft of the jack

Patent no. 836272/880537 of Federal Republic of
Germany and foreign patents

jack rack

pilot

dam-
per

23. Modern Neupert Jack
with "OK"-Silvertone Quill

6 Top regu-
lating screw

5

4 Tongue

3 spring

2 shaft

8
1

24. Jack with top regulation
(Neupert-Plastic-Jack)

1 pilo

XVI